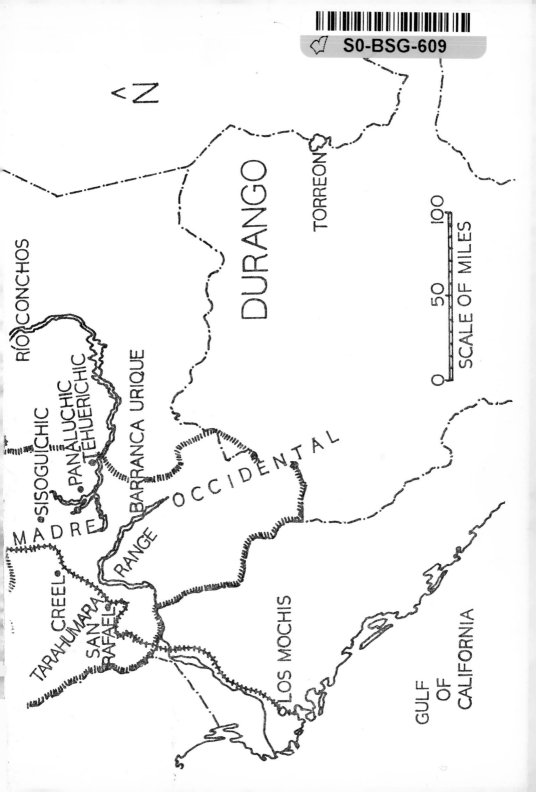

TARAHUMARA INDIANS

TARAHUMARA INDIANS

BY JONATHON F. CASSEL

The Naylor Company
Book Publishers of the Southwest
San Antonio, Texas

To my wife Estelle and son Jon —
My two favorite pack mules!

List of Illustrations

Picture section between pages xii and 1

Page 1   A study of privation and despair

Page 2   Top left: Baby with rickets — due to malnutrition

Top right: Woman with baby timidly walks past author's camp

Bottom left: Winners of a fifteen mile *rarahipa* (kickball race)

Bottom right: Woman's necklace is made of seeds and berries

Page 3   Top left: Shy tot warily watches strange camera

Top right: Chief poses with author's crossbow

Bottom left: Full tummy after feast begets rare smile

Bottom right: Young man watches activities at Creel station

Page 4   Top left: Author vainly tries to learn dance steps

Top right: Battered utensils salvaged from railroad site

Bottom left: Old primitive fiddles on violin he made

Bottom right: Author's wife (background) at *teshuino* party

Page 5   Top left: Dejected losers of *rarahipa* (kickball race)

Top right: Indian throws rock in game played like horseshoes

Bottom left: Chief Pat (right) and his dour predecessor
Bottom right: Cave dwellers at home

Page 6   Top left: Fall and winter cave home of Chief Pat

Top right: Thirteen-year-old wife with fourteen-year-old husband

Bottom left: Large and grotesque entrance to Indian cave

Bottom right: Indian on left is smoking wild tobacco cigaret

Page 7   Top left: Cave family; corn basket woven from river reeds

Top right: Crude wooden plow has no metal in construction

Bottom left: Hungry Indians await start of early-dawn feast

Bottom right: Artifacts and ore samples from Tarahumara-land

Page 8   Top left: Primitive hut is Chief Pat's summer home

Top right: Perch-like fish netted by Indians in Rio Conchos

Bottom left: Old man enjoys gift of pipe and foil of tobacco

Bottom right: Start of rain dance; note cross in left hand

Page 9   Top left: Sixteen-year-old Tarahumara in impressive pose

Top right: Start of *rarahipa*; note wooden kickball on ground

Bottom left: Rock apartment built within large cave

Bottom right: Indian with maguey roots — the Tarahumara's dulce

Page 10   Top left: Rio Urique flows through rock archway

Top right: Suspicious girl would not permit closer photo

Bottom left: Start of a new day; note cardboard sleeping pad

Bottom right: A helpless cripple; result of untreated disease

Page 11   Top left: Estelle and Jon examine Tarahumara burial cave

Top right: Cave home, 1,000 yards from Sisoguichic Mission

Bottom left: Clay jar serves as cooking pot or water jug

Bottom right: Tarahumara visits Creel railroad station

Page 12   Picturesque Tarahumara visits Sisoguichic Mission

viii

Introduction

Eons ago, volcanic forces spewed into being an awesome, forty-thousand-square-mile complex of deep and tortuous *barrancas,* or canyons. An interior part of the bristling Sierra Madre Occidental, this barranca region is known as the Tarahumara Range. Lying west of the city of Chihuahua, it is generally contained within the limits of the state of Chihuahua, Mexico.

The Tarahumara Range remains, to a great extent, unexplored and uncharted. Penetration and minor development has been restricted to the outer perimeter of this hostile and formidable wilderness.

The Chihuahua Pacific Railway spans the Sierra Madre and the northern reaches of the Tarahumara Range. Completed by Swiss engineers in 1961, the railroad twists and worms westward from the city of Chihuahua. It enters the Tarahumara country at the village of Creel, which is located at the threshold of mighty Barranca Urique, the principal canyon of the Tarahumara Range.

Eighty-nine tunnels and twenty-six bridges later, the railroad levels on the fertile coastal plains, and comes to an end at Los Mochis, on the Pacific coast. Aptly termed the "Railroad in the Sky," this rail line is indeed a tribute to modern engineering.

Aircraft landing facilities within the Tarahumara country are limited to two small, unimproved fields which can accommodate only light aircraft. One strip is located near Creel. The other is at Mission Sisoguichic. The treacherous air turbulence generated over the high plateaus and deep canyons makes flying in the barranca region extremely hazardous. It is not recommended except for the most experienced of pilots.

There are no highways in this wild land. Raw jeep trails, following the lines of least resistance, connect the several mission outposts with Creel. A few burro and foot trails lead into some of the canyons, extending but a short distance before dead-ending on the canyon floors.

Less than three hundred and fifty miles south of the border from El Paso, Texas, this vast wonderland of stark, raw beauty and vivid contrasts is the habitat of the Tarahumara cave dwellers, a distinct and unique tribe of Indians who live much as their ancestors did hundreds of years ago.

The Tarahumara's geographical environment

TOP LEFT: Baby with rickets — due to malnutrition

TOP RIGHT: Woman with baby timidly walks past author's camp

BOTTOM LEFT: Winners of a fifteen mile *rarahipa* (kickball race)

BOTTOM RIGHT: Woman's necklace is made of seeds and berries

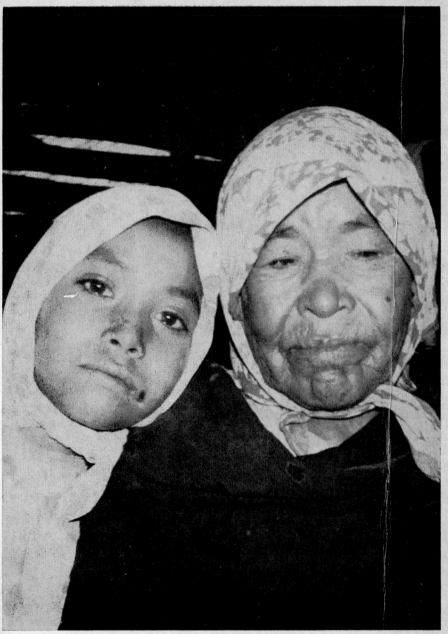

A study of privation and despair

The intervening centuries since Fonte's and Salvatierre's remarkable missionary efforts have noted little change in the status of the primitive Tarahumara. The endeavors of succeeding Jesuits were to suffer bitter reversals and many lengthy interruptions.

The few Tarahumara who had been converted soon forgot their Christian teachings. What had been learned was absorbed into their ancient tribal beliefs and swallowed in the depths of primeval superstitions.

In the nineteen hundreds, Jesuit missionary activities became alive once more. Progress has been painfully slow and difficult. Many obstacles block the way to a better life for the pitiful Tarahumara people. The greatest barriers are the Tarahumara themselves. The bitter experiences of bygone years have made them wary and suspicious of the ways of civilization.

has played a leading role in keeping the influence of the outside world at bay. In large measure, this unrelenting land is responsible for the Tarahumara being the most primitive of the North American Indians.

Because of its inaccessibility, and nature's built-in rigors, the ancient homeland of the Tarahumara cave people will remain a challenging wilderness for a long time to come. The Tarahumara Range guards its secrets jealously, and well.

The first recorded contact with the Tarahumara Indians was made in 1607, by Father Juan Fonte, a Jesuit missionary from Spain. This initial meeting took place at the southern extreme of the Tarahumara boundary.

In the early part of the seventeenth century, the Tarahumara of the northern barrancas received their first visitor from the outside world. Father Salvatierre, also a Jesuit missionary, entered the region where the village of Creel is now located. A few miles beyond he discovered the mighty and fantastic Barranca Urique.

This tremendous leftover of volcanic turmoil is commonly referred to as "Copper Canyon." The misnomer is due to the discovery and development of a large copper deposit by the early Spaniards.

TOP LEFT: Shy tot warily watches strange camera

TOP RIGHT: Chief poses with author's crossbow

BOTTOM LEFT: Full tummy after feast begets rare smile

BOTTOM RIGHT: Young man watches activities at Creel station

TOP LEFT: Author vainly tries to learn dance steps

TOP RIGHT: Battered utensils salvaged from railroad site

BOTTOM LEFT: Old primitive fiddles on violin he made

BOTTOM RIGHT: Author's wife (background) at *teshuino* party

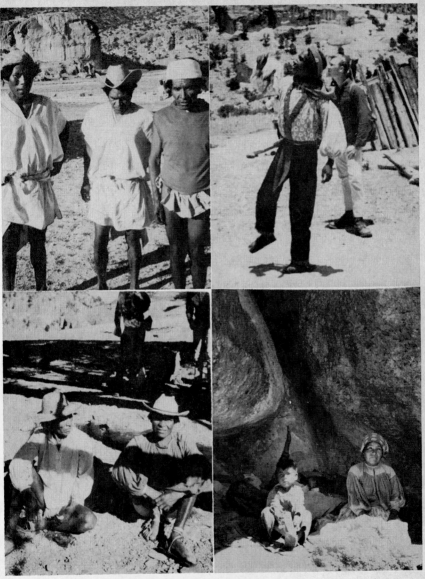

TOP LEFT: Dejected losers of *rarahipa* (kickball race)

TOP RIGHT: Indian throws rock in game played like horseshoes

BOTTOM LEFT: Chief Pat (right) and his dour predecessor

BOTTOM RIGHT: Cave dwellers at home

TOP LEFT: Fall and winter cave home of Chief Pat

BOTTOM LEFT: Large and grotesque entrance to Indian cave

TOP RIGHT: Thirteen-year-old wife with fourteen-year-old husband

BOTTOM RIGHT: Indian on left is smoking wild tobacco cigaret

TOP LEFT: Cave family; corn basket woven from river reeds

BOTTOM LEFT: Hungry Indians await start of early-dawn feast

TOP RIGHT: Crude wooden plow has no metal in construction

BOTTOM RIGHT: Artifacts and ore samples from Tarahumaraland

TOP LEFT: Primitive hut is Chief Pat's summer home

BOTTOM LEFT: Old man enjoys gift of pipe and foil of tobacco

TOP RIGHT: Perch-like fish netted by Indians in Rio Conchos

BOTTOM RIGHT: Start of rain dance; note cross in left hand

TOP LEFT: Sixteen-year-old Tarahumara in impressive pose

TOP RIGHT: Start of *rarahipa;* note wooden kickball on ground

BOTTOM LEFT: Rock apartment built within large cave

BOTTOM RIGHT: Indian with maguey root — the Tarahumara's dulce

TOP LEFT: Rio Urique flows through rock archway

TOP RIGHT: Suspicious girl would not permit closer photo

BOTTOM LEFT: Start of a new day; note cardboard sleeping pad

BOTTOM RIGHT: A helpless cripple; result of untreated disease

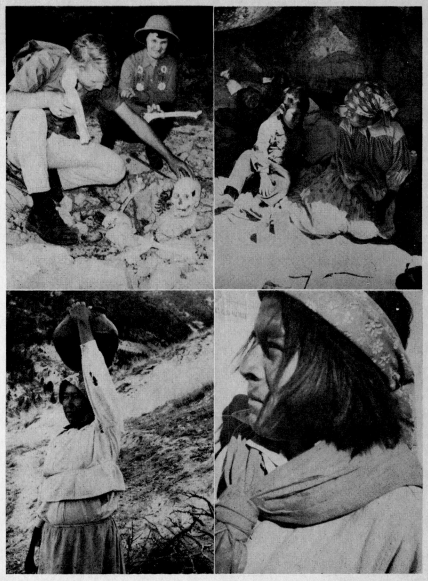

TOP LEFT: Estelle and Jon examine
Tarahumara burial cave

TOP RIGHT: Cave home, 1,000 yards
from Sisoguichic Mission

BOTTOM LEFT: Clay jar serves as cooking
pot or water jug

BOTTOM RIGHT: Tarahumara visits Creel
railroad station

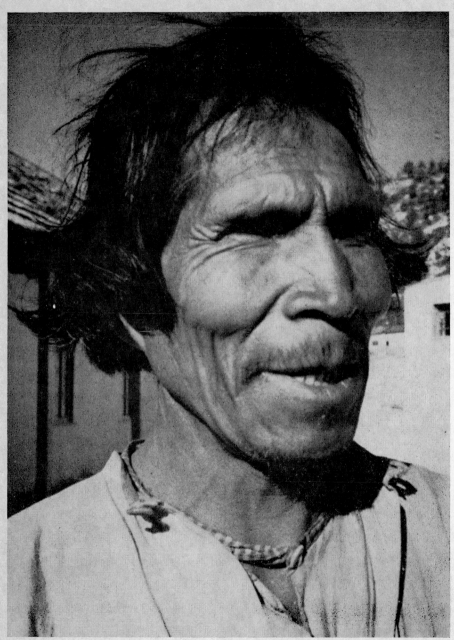

Picturesque Tarahumara visits Sisoguichic Mission

CHAPTER 1

The long months of
intensive physical fitness
training, and the weeks
of detailed planning and
preparation were over. My family and I announced our intention of backpacking into the wild

1

and forbidding Tarahumara Range of Mexico.

One of our objectives would be to explore an unknown portion of the mysterious Barranca Urique — a tremendous chasm four and one-half times larger, and two thousand feet deeper, than the Grand Canyon of the Colorado. If our efforts proved successful, we would be the first non-Indian family to do so.

The primary purpose of our adventure, however, was to penetrate the interior of the canyon country where, hopefully, we would study and photograph the Tarahumara Indian cave dwellers. This, too, would be an American family "first."

Our plans to go prowling on foot in the Tarahumara country created an immediate stir of concern among friends and strangers alike. They were in general agreement that we would never come back alive. The question most often asked of us was, "Why must you go?"

My personal interest in primitive peoples extends from my childhood days in northern Montana. With Indian reservations near our sprawling ranch, it was only natural that many of my friends were Indian lads.

Swimming and fishing in the murky waters of the Milk River, hunting coyotes and jack-rabbits on the rolling prairie — these and other

2

normal boyhood activities with my Indian friends gave me an understanding of our bona fide Americans which few are privileged to receive.

My youthful interests in Indians carried over into adulthood. In my travels, particularly in the far-flung islands and land masses of the Pacific, I never ignored an opportunity to visit and observe aborigines, whether they were Polynesian islanders, headhunters of New Guinea, or the aborigines of Australia.

The Sierra Madre Occidental had beckoned me for years, but my military career prevented my heeding her call. After my retirement from the U.S. Army, I heard vague, exciting tales about the Tarahumara cave dwellers. I was now free to satisfy my inherent curiosity and investigate the Sierra Madre, and the Tarahumara, the most primitive of the North American Indians.

My petite, blonde wife, Estelle, and fifteen-year-old son, Jon, insisted on accompanying me on my adventure. We have always been a close-knit family. Unlike mine, their motives for wanting to go along were quite fundamental. Backed by a rare courage and determination, they were willing to dare extreme hardship and danger for the sake of "togetherness."

Because this was to be a family venture, I received several highly critical telephone calls. Very

3

few were intended to bolster my courage. One man, calling long-distance, scolded me severely. "I read in the paper that you are going into the Tarahumara country without a gun," he said. "I spent many years in northern Mexico, and I heard terrible stories about those Indians. You are crazy to take your wife and young son in there without the protection of a firearm."

It was my firm belief that we could establish a common bond of friendship with the Tarahumara solely on the basis of "family meets family." The presence of a gun would only create an atmosphere of suspicion and danger. Our total armament would consist of a pair of heavy Bowie knives, a crossbow, and a quiver of hunting arrows.

As I had hoped, the crossbow was to prove a real "door-opener" for us. Skilled in the use of their own crude longbows, the Tarahumara were extremely interested in the strange crossbow, and were amazed at its performance.

On the evening prior to our departure we held a final inspection and weigh-in of our individual packs, and allied camping gear. Traveling on foot in an unknown wilderness of mountains and canyons made it imperative that we not be overloaded. On the other hand, if we failed to include the minimum needs of food, medical

4

items, and other vital supplies, our ultimate defeat would be certain — and almost surely disastrous.

In addition to our own supplies, we stowed in the packs an assortment of articles which we would give to the Indians. There were packets of needles, spools of thread, and small bars of soap for the women; shrill toy whistles, tiny harmonicas, and hard candies for the children; salt, bright red bandannas, and a dozen rat traps for the men.

Rat traps may seem to be odd items for gifts. But to a primitive who must rely upon crude snares to catch small game animals, a rat trap can appear like a gift from the gods.

Rigid adherence to a carefully planned physical training routine conditioned us for the hard tasks ahead. For six months we had averaged a minimum hike of at least ten miles per day — rain or shine. In the final stages of our physical training, we included backpacks on our overland treks.

None of us are physically large, yet Estelle carried a pack weighing twenty-five pounds. Jon was to bear a forty-five pound load. The sixty-five pounds I allocated to myself was to eventually prove an overload.

In addition to the foregoing pack loads, items such as the camera, water canteens, fifty feet of manila rope, crossbow, quiver of arrows, Bowie knives, and other paraphernalia had to be carried on our persons. No space was wasted. Even our pockets were loaded.

On June 1, 1966, we stepped off the Chihuahua Pacific Railroad passenger train as it stopped briefly at San Rafael, Chihuahua. It was seven o'clock in the morning. The rising sun was probing long, reddish fingers amid the rocky crags and cliffs that surround San Rafael, dispersing lingering pockets of post-dawn shadows.

San Rafael is located about twelve miles west of Divisidero Barrancas, and approximately eighteen miles from the west rim of Barranca Urique, our immediate objective. The tiny village of ramshackle huts was born when the railroad was laid through this section of the Tarahumara wilderness. The sole reason for its existence is the nearby forests, the source of railroad ties used on the line.

The population is less than one hundred strong (not counting the many mongrel dogs) and consists mainly of Mexican railroad hands and tie-splitters. They are augmented by a few Tarahumara Indian laborers who traded in their wild freedom for a pick and shovel.

San Rafael's center of activities is the railroad station. Long before an incoming train's demented whistle echoes shrilly among the mute peaks, the small waiting room is aburst with excited humanity. As the coaches grind to a stop there is a sudden, furious exodus from the waiting room. Young and old spill out onto the platform. The adults mill about, craning their necks and wildly waving their arms at the staring faces of the passengers, none of whom they know. The children run madly along the string of coaches, begging the curious travelers to buy proffered bits of shiny quartz and crystal ore.

Tourists do not get off the train at San Rafael. There are no accommodations, not even a café. We were objects of great curiosity and excitement as we shouldered our way through the milling throng and entered the station. There we met Señor Mendez, the station agent. Our knowledge of Spanish being poor, at best, we were delighted that Señor Mendez spoke a halting form of English, painfully learned through a correspondence course.

We explained to the kindly señor that we were going to explore Barranca Urique, and that we were in need of a competent guide. "Señor," he said. "I beg to tell you — no one, except a few Mexican men, have ever been to the bottom of Barranca Urique. Not in this area." He looked at Estelle and Jon. "Maybe, Señor, you should enter Urique back at Creel. There you will find some trails. Barranca Urique, in this area you want to go is too dangerous. Especially for a woman, and a boy."

I informed him of our determination to go into the great canyon at the point we had planned, and again asked if a guide might be available. Señor Mendez sighed and shrugged his shoulders in resignation. He said that a Señor Salas, a local citizen and an official guide for the Mexican government, would be happy to guide us. However, Señor Salas was not at home.

"Do not worry," said Señor Mendez. "His son, Rafael, will guide you. Yes, he is qualified. He and his father have made many difficult trips into the barrancas." A runner was dispatched to fetch Rafael.

The messenger returned with our prospective guide at his side. Skeptically, we studied sixteen-year-old Rafael. He appeared not at all like an experienced guide. A thin, wiry lad with darting and inquisitive black eyes, his mop of unruly black hair had never met a comb. A frayed, blue-plaid shirt draped loosely over his slight shoulders. The faded and multi-patched denim trousers were folded tightly to narrow hips by a belt of dirty rope. His grimy feet were harnessed to heelless leather sandals by twisted rawhide thongs.

8

Through the interpretive efforts of the station master we quizzed Rafael at great length. The boy's calm and logical answers eased most of the initial doubts as to his abilities. I was sure that his tender years would prove no barrier. For Rafael, and others nurtured in this isolated environment, childhood is a fleeting luxury. The constant struggle for survival brings an early maturity.

We employed Rafael as our guide, with the understanding that he must provide his own food supply and whatever else he might need for a week's stay in the big canyon. He readily agreed and ran to his home.

In a few minutes he returned, carrying a ragged serape and a yellowed cloth sack filled with tortilla flour. He was accompanied by a Tarahumara Indian youth whom he introduced as "Mateo," a name probably bestowed upon him at a mission.

Mateo spoke no English. His knowledge of Spanish was nil. Seventeen years old, short, powerful and stocky, he was dressed much like Rafael. The chief difference was his sandals. Laced to his feet with buckskin strings, the sandals were crudely shaped pieces of rubber tread cut from a discarded automobile tire. (This mode of footgear is not uncommon among the peasants of Latin American countries.)

9

Mateo was shy and reserved. Whenever we glanced his way he flashed us a quick, wide-toothed smile. It was quite evident that Mateo expected to join our party. He, too, carried a serape over one shoulder, and a sack of corn flour.

Rafael matter-of-factly stated that Mateo was indeed going with us. He explained that, being a native of the barrancas, Mateo would know where to find the all-important springs of water along our route. Further, argued Rafael, his friend was strong "like a burro." He could help carry our packs. Rafael presented his companion's case well. Mateo was hired.

There was one final interruption before we left San Rafael. Another stranger sauntered casually into our midst. He cooly inspected Estelle, Jon, and me, wrinkled his moist nose, and barked his approval, before sitting on his haunches to await further development. Named "Tigre," he was a three-quarter coyote dog belonging to Rafael. Tigre, of course, was invited to join the expedition.

At last organized and assembled, we waved good-bye to the motley crowd gathered to stare and wonder at the strange *Norte Americanos*. Single file, we trooped up a steep hill to a wooded region above the village. At the top of the hill

10

we paused for a final look back. The twin ribbon of railroad steel glistened below. Its impact was tremendous, for it was the last link with the world we knew. None of us voiced our qualms as we settled into our packs and moved forward to meet the challenge of the unknown.

We were at an elevation of approximately seven thousand feet above sea level. Weather conditions were ideal, and the going was easy. The sky was a sapphire blue, without a hint of clouds. The sun was friendly and pleasantly warm. A bashful breeze flirted with the elusive, fragrant aromas of spruce, cedar, and pine.

Within a few miles this Utopian condition came to an abrupt and permanent end. From then on, it was a constant and agonizing struggle with a virgin wilderness, devoid of any but the faintest of game trails.

I had with me an operational navigation chart that covered the northern portion of the Sierra Madre Occidental. Prepared for the Mexican government by the United States Air Force, this aerial map, and a lensatic compass, enabled me to keep a close check on our position. For obvious reasons it was imperative that I maintain constant and correct bearings.

We soon appreciated the value of Mateo's

presence. He always seemed to know when one of us was tiring. At such times, he would walk to one of us and without a word, relieve that person of his burdensome pack. Usually that one of us was me. I was awed by the Indian lad's remarkable strength and stamina. Light-footed, without effort, he would carry my heavy pack for miles, never once giving any indication of tiring.

The terrain leading to the west rim of Barranca Urique is strewn with huge boulders and countless rocks. There are few open valleys or gentle slopes. We scrambled up steep canyon walls, only to find still other rocky escarpments awaiting us at the summits.

We had looked forward to coming upon our first Tarahumara Indian community. We were to be disappointed. The harsh and unyielding barrancas will not support human life in a societal grouping. The estimated 42,000 Tarahumara people are scattered widely throughout the canyon complex.

It was midafternoon of that first day that we saw a Tarahumara Indian — a woman. She was about a quarter of a mile from us, standing by a rock hut that blended into the barren hillside like a careless heap of stones.

We pressed forward with great anticipation

12

and excitement. Before we could come within camera range, the woman darted into the hut. She quickly emerged, carrying an infant in her arms. Tagging close at her heels was a second child, perhaps five years of age.

The woman walked several paces from the hut and stopped. Erect and graceful, she gazed at us for a brief moment. Clutching her baby tightly to her breast she fled like a frightened deer, the other child running at her side. Long, jet black hair streaming behind her, the woman swiftly vanished in a nearby jumble of massive boulders. We did not see her again.

Caution dictated that we not approach the hut any closer. It was unlikely that the Indian woman lived there alone with her two children. There was the distinct possibility that her husband lurked within, or nearby. I had no intention of walking into trouble, and we bypassed the dwelling.

We saw several more Tarahumara men and women that afternoon. The results were the same. They ran from us, furtively glancing over their shoulders at the intruding white strangers. The fact that Mateo, one of their kind, called friendly greetings to them apparently made no soothing impression upon the frightened Indians.

June is the hottest and driest month in the

Tarahumara Range. During this time, flowing streams are practically nonexistent, except for a few spring-fed streams that flow in the bottoms of the deeper canyons. Until we should reach Rio Urique, our only water source would be the rare constant-level springs we might locate along the way.

Contained in shallow, bowl-shaped depressions in the solid rock formations which dominate the barrancas, the water lies but a few inches below the surface of the bowls, and is nonflowing.

The Tarahumara endeavor to protect these springs from despoiling animals and birds, and from the evaporative effect of the extreme heat. The bowls, or depressions, are so cleverly covered with slabs of stone, pieces of broken tree limbs, or clumps of heavy brush that detection is very difficult. In fact, the uninitiated stands practically on top of a hidden spring and never knows that the water he seeks is immediately at hand.

Although we conserved our water and drank sparingly, our canteens were frequently empty. Several times our need for water became critical. But for the unerring ability of Mateo to lead us to a hidden spring, our situation would have become serious indeed.

The finding of a hidden spring was always the occasion for an extended cooling-off rest period.

We would slowly drink the clear, delicious water, which was quite cool, in spite of the blazing 100 plus degrees reflected from the sun-tortured rocks all about us.

Once our thirst was satisfied, we would fill our canteens and pour the water over our heads and clothing, then lie down and rest. Rafael would do the same. Mateo, the boy of iron, would drink but a few sips of water, and disdain to so much as bathe his face.

The constant-level springs are unusual. The capacity of the shallow depressions is seldom more than a gallon or two of water. As the water is removed, such as in the filling of a canteen, the level drops to a mere cupful in the bottom of the bowl. Within a few minutes, however, the water returns to its normal level, approximately two inches below the rim of the depression.

It was nearing sundown when we arrived at the west rim of Barranca Urique. Our first task was to gather a large quantity of wood for the campfire, which was to be kept burning throughout the night. Supper posed no great chore, for we were too exhausted to bother with anything more complicated in preparation than hot soup.

The rocky, sloping terrain prevented the pitching of our small tent. Jon and I each had a lightweight woolen blanket. Estelle enjoyed the comparative luxury of a thin sleeping bag. Mateo and Rafael bedded down near the fire, rolled up in their bedraggled serapes. The rock ground was most uncomfortable, and the crawling ants and inquisitive, unidentified bugs did little to promote restful sleep.

Little Tigre, the coyote-dog, had been ignored all day by Rafael, his master. Estelle won the little fellow's devotion by a few pats on his head, plus some small snacks of food. During the evening meal, Rafael neglected to give the dog some of his corn tortilla he had cooked over the campfire. Estelle gave Tigre his supper — a share of her soup. He showed his appreciation by standing guard at the foot of her sleeping bag, alert to warn her of every sound in the surrounding darkness.

Near midnight, we were awakened by Tigre's low, menacing growls. On the perimeter of the fire's flickering light was a large cougar. Standing broadside, he presented a magnificent picture of poised, naked power. The great, tawny head turned toward us, and the yellow eyes directed their chilling glare at Tigre, whose ferocious growls quickly subsided to frightened whimpers. After a few moments, his curiosity satisfied, the big cat flowed quickly and gracefully into the darkness.

16

Shortly after two o'clock in the morning Tigre awakened us again. I flashed my electric lantern in the direction of his taut interest. The bright beam illuminated a brace of startled Indians in a nearby grove of trees. They froze in their tracks for a brief moment, then melted swiftly out of the flood of light.

The Indians I had known in the past did not travel about at night. Were the Tarahumara merely passing by us in the darkness? Or were they scouting our campsite with mischief in mind? For the first time, serious doubts about the wisdom of our family adventure assailed me. I was wide awake the remainder of that long night, recalling the many dire warnings I had received from the people back home.

When we began the long and hazardous descent into Barranca Urique, the rising sun was peering red-eyed, and already angry, over the lacerated eastern rim of the canyon walls. The magnificent, early-morning beauty of the raw wilderness below us made me forget the fears that had bedeviled me throughout the previous night.

The topography and the scenery of the barrancas changes rapidly. On our approach to the west rim of Urique Canyon we had walked through occasional forests of pine, spruce, fir, and

17

cedar. As we started down into the canyon, the forests were replaced by a wide assortment of oak trees. Some of the types were barren of leaves, not to wear a new dress of green until after the end of the rainy season in late September.

The oaks soon gave way to a shallow belt of dense brush and stubby scrub oak. Below this, we encountered scattered clumps of cactus, interspersed with patches of dried and lifeless bunchgrass. A few hundred yards farther down, nearly all vegetation disappeared, leaving only a grotesque confusion of dangling precipices, towering crags, deep chasms, and rock-filled gorges.

We discovered a hot spring. The frothy, boiling water gurgled over the rim of the rock caldron and steamed its way into a nearby fissure before it had a chance to cool. We wished we had at least a dozen eggs to cook in the boiling water.

In the various levels of the canyons we saw many Tarahumara cave dwellings, none with tenants. During the months of April through October, the Indians, with a few exceptions, leave their winter homes in the caves and move to the higher regions of the canyons, and to the plateaus, where topsoil can be found that will grow corn, or maize, the Indians' food staple.

The caves, formed by centuries of erosive wind and water action on the soft, volcanic rock,

18

are generally shallow in depth. Many of the caves are quite large in actual floor space, often in excess of four hundred square feet, with ceiling heights of ten feet or more.

Utilization of these natural caves by the Tarahumara is quite logical, since they possess neither the knowledge nor the tools to construct a dwelling nearly so practical. The rock and log huts and the simple pole lean-tos in which they live during the summer months would not suffice as winter shelters.

CHAPTER 2

It was late afternoon
when we had our first
full view of the beautiful
Río Urique. We stood
on the edge of a steep bluff, overlooking the
canyon floor. From this vantage point it appeared

21

that the river was less than a mile distant. We were spurred on with renewed energy. Within a few minutes we should reach our goal.

As it developed, however, we still had not learned well the lessons that the great, unflexible barranca had tried to teach us for two long and exhaustive days. The expected one mile stretched to at least five. Four hours after first sighting it, we stumbled to the river's edge. It was fifteen minutes before eight o'clock. The hot, brassy sun was dipping below the western parapets of Urique.

We had accomplished our secondary mission — to be the first non-Indian family to stand in this unique area of North America, two thousand feet deeper than the Grand Canyon of the Colorado. Shedding our wretched packs, our first impulse was to leap and shout for joy.

Our supreme elation died aborning. The eerie, silent splendor of the surrounding scene subdued, even frightened, us. The vast chaos of prehistoric volcanic madness imparted the feeling that, somehow, we had been transported to an awesome, unreal world, far removed from our own. In a very real sense, we had. Civilization was many miles behind us. Should misfortune befall us in this hostile, mysterious region, we could expect no help. At this instant, God was close enough to touch.

22

Recovering some of our composure, we searched for a place to spend the night. We found a cave
a short distance from the river and deposited our
packs and gear inside the gaping entrance. A rock
metate and pieces of whitened bone scattered about
the cave floor indicated that we were borrowing
an Indian family's winter home.

It was fast becoming dusk. Jon and I wanted
to refresh ourselves with a swim before supper.
We found a spot where the water was deep and
quiet, and began to shed our clothes. Mateo ran
to us, waving his arms and talking rapidly. After
a great deal of sign language, Mateo, with an
assist from Rafael, managed to convey to us a
picture of a voracious killer fish that lurked in
the deep water. My first thought was of the
dreaded piranha. The swim was promptly can-
celled.

We subsequently tried to observe this strange
fish described by Mateo. I saw one in a deep pool.
About six inches long, it had a jutting lower jaw
that appeared to have a row of short, needlelike
teeth. In the brief moment that I saw the fish,
it seemed that the lower half, or belly, was nearly
transparent. It is perhaps significant that we failed
to see any other type of fish, or minnows, in the
Río Urique — including frogs or tadpoles.

During our night's stay in the fire-blackened

cave, we were invaded by hordes of thirsty mosquitos, prowling ants, and the stifling heat which continued to radiate from the surrounding rocks and cliffs.

On the morning of June 3, we moved upriver, exploring the canyon floor. The serpentine river proved to be an energy-consuming obstacle. Several times we were barred from forward progress by steep cliffs plunging into the deep water of the river. With the possibility of cannibal fish in mind, we sought narrow and shallow depths where we could wade to the opposite bank in safety.

The fordings were not without humorous incidents. On one occasion, we were crossing the river by jumping from boulder to boulder. Near the middle of the stream, where the water was quite deep, Estelle misjudged her leap and disappeared beneath the surface. She cannot swim, but she managed to hold our only camera above the water.

Trusting that she could hold her breath for several seconds, I first retrieved the precious camera, before pulling her, sputtering and bedraggled, beside me on a boulder. Always the good sport, she laughed with the rest of us and said, "I'm glad we aren't going anywhere tonight — my hair must be a sight!"

From shortly after sunrise until early dusk, the rock-walled confines of Barranca Urique were like a coke oven. The baleful sun, a furnace in the cloudless sky, sapped our energy. I was thankful that we had included salt tablets in our medical supplies. Rafael, too, was nearly overcome by the heat. Mateo, true to Tarahumara form, remained undaunted and undamaged.

We probed the mysteries of Urique northward for about five miles. We passed through areas of dense, bamboolike thickets, where we flushed large numbers of brightly colored parrots. They flew downriver raucously screaming their displeasure of our intrusion.

Several times we found jaguar tracks at the river's edge, where the nocturnal beasts had paused for a drink during the previous night. Estelle and Jon saw one of the powerful cats standing on a ledge, high on the side of a rock cliff. I did not see it. By the time I had located the ledge, the animal had gone.

Tropical gardens are tucked away in the gaping mouths of the large feeder-canyons which open on Urique's floor. Groves of bananas, guava, papaya, mango, and avocado beckoned us. The citrus family was represented by limes, lemons, and oranges. Unfortunately for us, the fruit was green, not to ripen until quite late in the year.

25

Mateo and Rafael filled their pockets with the small, green limes, which they chewed with relish as they walked.

Wild tobacco, eagerly sought by the Tarahumara, grows in some areas of the barrancas, including Urique. A wide variety of orchid plants are native to the region. (The Indians have an unusual application for the bulbs, which will be described later.)

Unknown species of gorgeous flowers in both bright and pastel shades blossomed in the tropical vegetation areas. Hummingbirds darted amid the blooms, busily probing every flower.

Although we saw none, we were later informed that monkeys can be found in Barranca Urique's secluded tropical gardens.

During our descent into Urique we had noticed a virtual absence of bird and animal life. This might be attributed to the dry season, or, more likely, to the constantly foraging Indians. Perhaps we frightened the wildlife away. It was impossible for us to travel quietly. The creak and thump of our packs, the jangling of loosely hanging equipment, and the solid slap of boot leather on the uncushioned rock surface would certainly alert all birds and game that might be ahead of us.

Barranca Urique is rich in valuable mineral and gem deposits. Reportedly, the Indians have brought diamonds out of the canyon. As we threaded our way through the canyon, we picked up samples of quartz, crystal, gold, silver, and copper ores, and opals.

We had expected that our packs would become lighter with each passing day. The addition of the mineral samples plus the accumulation of bulky Indian artifacts only increased our heavy burdens.

Near the end of the third day we started our return journey to San Rafael. Not wanting to backtrack, we searched the forbidding canyon walls for a place to begin our ascent. About a mile from our position on the river we spotted a small hut. It was squatted between two vertebrae of a spiny ridge, about six hundred feet above the canyon floor. The precipitous ridge appeared to be the only likely route for us to begin our climb to the west rim.

The climb to the hut, plus the past three days' strenuous activities, exacted their toll. We were utterly exhausted. Even Mateo, the indestructible, showed definite signs of weariness. Little Tigre, too tired to eat his supper, stretched his small, gaunt frame on the rocks of the hut yard and immediately fell asleep.

We examined the interior of the rock hovel. Fresh scuff marks in the dust and dirt of the

27

floor and a bed of new wood ashes indicated that Indians had recently been there. We had not seen any Tarahumara since leaving the upper levels of Barranca Urique. But I knew that the Indians, from distant and hidden vantage points, had been, and still were, watching our every move.

The interior furnishings of the hut were typically few — a metate and several bowls made from the lower halves of large gourds. The lone exception was a large tribal drum leaning against a wall. The drum frame, a six-inch width of cedar strip, was bent to form a crude circle about thirty inches in diameter. Over this was stretched two pieces of untanned deerskin, one on each side.

The skins were tightly stretched on the facings, meeting at the edges of the drum, where they were interlaced with strips of rawhide. Beside the drum was a short length of wood. It was wadded at one end with a stiffly dried animal hide. This served as the drumstick.

We bedded down for the night outside the hut. Jon found a comfortable spot parallel to the edge of the cliff fronting the hut. Prior to settling down for the night, he constructed a retaining wall of rocks.

At dawn, we enjoyed a leisurely breakfast. None of us were eager to resume the ascent, which

28

was to prove much more difficult than our descent. The terrain was steeper and presented more difficult obstacles. We were compelled to make many a painful detour.

The vengeful sun, the unrelenting canyon, and our pack loads sapped our reserve energy, upon which we had already drawn heavily. Estelle, Jon, and I looked like sunburned castaways. Rafael and Mateo showed the strain, and little Tigre must have regretted becoming a part of our expedition.

Two-thirds of the way toward the top of the west rim, we stopped at a small ravine where we decided to camp. Leaving Estelle to rest in the shade of a huge boulder, the rest of us walked down a dry stream bed in a search for water.

Mateo, of course, was the one who finally located the hidden spring. I noticed something quite different about this water hole. Someone, or something, had only recently visited this spring. It was cleverly concealed with brush, but there were the telltale signs of water having been splashed on the rock surface adjacent to the small pool. Beads of moisture still clung to the porous rock. My immediate thought was of Indians. The second thought that worried me was Estelle, alone, a considerable distance above us where we had left her.

I fitted an arrow to the crossbow and walked swiftly but quietly up the ravine, carefully picking my way among the labyrinth of rocks. Reaching the place where we had left Estelle, I froze in amazement. She was standing a few feet from the side of the boulder where she had been sitting, bravely making a very nervous sign-talk to a silent, stony-faced Tarahumara Indian.

The Indian turned and watched me warily as I confronted him. For a few highly charged seconds we studied each other. His attention shifted to the leveled crossbow. As his piercing black eyes, sunken deeply behind high cheeks, lifted from the readied weapon to again lock with mine, I could sense his apprehension. I lowered the bow and extended my hand in a gesture of friendship.

The Tarahumara slowly reached his right hand toward mine. Gently, but quickly, he stroked my open palm with the tips of his fingers, then let his hand drop to his side. This curious, seldom-used manner of greeting — almost like a feathery caress, is typical of the Tarahumara.

After his fingers had touched my palm, the Indian's fixed, deeply bronzed face creased into a wide, snaggletoothed smile. He pointed to Estelle, and then to me. Still grinning, he waved an arm down toward the dry stream bed where the boys were coming into view.

30

Giving each of them the caressing finger stroke on the palm, he then turned toward a high crest we had been climbing before coming to the ravine. As he repeatedly pointed toward the distant ridge, and back to us, we came to understand. He had been watching us since early afternoon. It was he who had spilled the water around the hidden spring.

The Indian and Mateo held a short but rapid conversation. Then Mateo and Rafael had an exchange of Spanish and Tarahumara. After a few minutes of frantic sign language between all of us, the central message filtered through. The Indian wanted us to accompany him to his home.

In the excitement of our initial meeting, I had not noticed the Indian's physical characteristics, nor manner of dress. Straight, jet black hair, tinged with wide streaks of grey, fell loosely over his shoulders. His high cheekbones made me think of the Apache. He appeared to be quite old, perhaps sixty years or more. Actually, he had not yet attained forty-five years, the average life-span of the Tarahumara people.

His upper garment was tattered and threadbare. What was left of it was very dirty. The ragged lower edge of the one-piece, buttonless shirt met the upper portion of his novel loin cloth. Worn like a diaper, it was ingeniously tied at the

31

front, with a corner of the cloth hanging loosely down the Indian's rear. His thin, corded legs were bare, as were his feet.

The Tarahumara's lean, whipcord body and his erect posture made him appear much taller than his five and one-half feet. As we followed him over the rocky, uneven terrain, I was struck by the youthful grace and ease with which he walked.

The Indian's home was located on a slope, overlooking a wide and barren valley. Our approach to the hut led us through the middle of a small field of stunted and wilted corn which was struggling to stay alive in the arid, shalelike volcanic soil.

Ironically, the arrival of the July rains, which are normally heavy, would result in much of the meagre corn crop being washed away into the canyons. This would become a tragic loss. Every year, many of the Tarahumara suffer death by starvation.

The Indian's primitive hut was a ten by ten feet square structure of crisscrossed small logs. The wide gaps between the logs were unchinked. Made of poles and tree branches, the flat roof was covered with brush and stones. There were no windows. A narrow opening, without a door, served as the entryway.

32

Our host's wife, daughter, and four grandchildren (two boys and two girls) were nervously clustered in front of the hut. The females were dressed alike, in two-piece, coarse cotton dresses. Loose-fitting, buttonless, with unevenly spaced stitching, the clumsily fashioned garments extended nearly to the wearers' bare feet. Like their grandfather, the boys were garbed in tattered shirts and diapered loincloths.

We had rather expected the old Indian to introduce us to his waiting family. However, he completely ignored them and entered the hut, leaving all of us to our own devices. (We would learn that such social behavior is normal with the Tarahumara. Taciturn and reserved, they waste no time or words on personal introductions and chitchat.)

Getting acquainted with the quietly hostile family was an experience. Words were futile. Rafael's Spanish was no help. Mateo could communicate with them, but was unable to interpret the results to us.

Only after we rummaged in our packs and produced pieces of hard candy did we make a favorable impression. When the strange, sweet candy melted in their mouths, the impassive, inscrutable faces broke into illuminating smiles of approval. Their taut suspicion of us also melted.

33

The phlegmatic old squaw, whom we named "Grandma," was nearly forty-five years old. Like "Grandpa," she was almost toothless. Her long, black hair was held away from the deeply lined leathery face by a red bandannalike cloth, knotted beneath her chin.

If she was curious about her strange visitors from an unknown world, she failed to show it. Except for the brief smile after tasting the candy, she remained expressionless. Never once did the old woman utter a single word in our presence.

The most compelling feature about Grandma was her large black eyes. Their haunted depths revealed many things — the privations and hunger of the past, and the hopelessness of the future.

The daughter, fourteen years of age, was married. She had no children. Her fifteen-year-old husband worked as a laborer on the railroad, eighteen miles away. He came home at the end of each working day, traveling the thirty-six-mile round trip on foot.

The four grandchildren ranged in age from four to eleven years. They belonged to a son. He and his wife were temporarily away in another area of the canyon.

The eldest boy and girl were aloof, unwilling to break through the wall of strangeness between us. Throughout our visit they remained at a dis-

34

tance, discreetly watching our every move. The two youngest children were different. After the first critical moments of our meeting, they behaved much like any other youngsters when unexpected company drops in.

Delightfully curious, they constantly bubbled around us and our strange possessions. We encouraged their heartwarming behavior by frequent stuffings of their drawn cheeks with candy.

The physical scars of their miserable existence were plain to see. Uncontrolled childhood diseases had left permanent marks on the gaunt faces. The distended bellies were mute testimony to the effects of malnutrition.

These unfortunate Indians were typical of all we would later meet in the barranca country. Although this particular family had the assistance of a wage-earning son-in-law, they were the rare exception, rather than the rule. The few pennies the son-in-law was able to earn could do very little to alleviate their abject poverty.

Estelle, Jon, and I entered the hut, leaving the children outside, ecstatically blowing loud discords from the small harmonicas we had given each of them. Grandpa was sitting cross-legged on the dirt floor, staring hard at nothing. He looked up as we entered. I gave him my pipe and last packet of tobacco.

35

I shall never forget the pure joy and contentment that spread over his face as he puffed greedily on the pipe, and found it good — much tastier than the acrid smoke from wild tobacco rolled in a shred of dried corn husk. Grinning broadly, Grandpa left the hut to sit outside on a rock and enjoy his new-found treat.

Conditions inside the hut were appalling. In one corner a wood fire was burning. The surging smoke engulfed the small room before streaming outside through the gaps in the log walls and the holes in the sagging roof.

Several fire-blackened tin cans were lying about on the pulverized dirt floor. Brought from the site of the railroad by the son-in-law, these grime-encrusted and badly bent cans were the only utensils the family possessed. Except for the rock metate, a large gourd converted to a water jug, and a large, handmade clay pot, the room was devoid of any other furnishings.

I watched Grandma as she prepared the evening meal. Kneeling on the floor, she bent over the metate and, with a square piece of stone, crushed a couple of handfuls of corn into a coarse meal.

The daughter mixed the meal with water and kneaded the mixture on the metate until it formed into a doughy mass. The water that was squeezed from the mixture ran down the sloped stone into a tin can. This liquid would be consumed by the Indians for any possible nourishment it might contain.

After the kneading process the dough was handed to Grandma. She pulled small globs from it and shaped them into small, very thin patties. These were tossed on the coals of the fire. When the corn cakes were sufficiently scorched, they were plucked from the coals and stacked on the ground beside the daughter.

Each member of the family received one of the corn cakes. Our party was invited to partake of the Tarahumara supper (actually, their only meal of the day). Mateo and Rafael accepted the invitation eagerly. They gulped their portion of cake, and would gladly have eaten more. Estelle, Jon, and I took a wee bite out of courtesy. It tasted quite good, though the corn cakes had no salt or other seasonings. If we had not watched the food being prepared and cooked, perhaps we might have eaten more.

Later in the evening, we built a fire near the hut and prepared our own supper of beef stew. The Tarahumara were reluctant to accept a portion of the stew, but we persuaded them to taste it. There was no indication that they liked our civilized recipe of stewed meat — possibly because of the unfamiliar seasonings.

37

The sun was low when we finished our supper. There was still time to demonstrate the crossbow before dusk. I set a small piece of wood at a distance of about twenty yards. When I triggered the arrow, Grandpa and the children hurried to the target. The old Indian was visibly excited when he saw that the two-inch steel arrowhead had disappeared into the semihardwood target.

After darkness, I entertained the family with renditions of Spanish and American folk music on my harmonica. They were more interested in the mechanics of the instrument than they were with my interpretation of Brahm's "Lullaby." Grandpa listened for a time with disjointed interest, then abruptly arose from his squatted position on the ground and disappeared into the darkness.

In a few minutes he returned, carrying a handmade replica of a violin. A remarkably accurate copy, it was designed from cedar which had been rasped to the desired shape and thickness with pieces of rough quartz. The strings were thin, rusty wires, procured from a mission area.

The bow, also of cedar, was strung with human hair — probably Grandma's. (Strands of yucca fibre are also used by the Tarahumara as bowstrings.) To maintain tautness, a small stone, inserted under the bowstrings, was simply pushed toward the butt end of the bow.

38

The instrument's belly and back were secured to the wall by a glue made from the wild orchid bulb. Grandpa's violin, which is now my prized possession, is quite old. Yet, the unusual glue is the strongest part of the instrument's body.

It is not known when the violin first fell into Tarahumara hands. Perhaps it was introduced by the early Jesuits, or the Spanish soldiers of the day. It is strange indeed that a primitive people who do not fashion the simplest of tools, or an arrowhead, can faithfully copy a violin. To my knowledge, the only other musical device the Indians make is a simple flute, made from bamboo-like reeds that grow in the deeper canyons.

Grandpa obliged us with a rendition of Tarahumara music. He fiddled with his right hand, holding the instrument against his chest with the left. There was no fingering of the strings, only a monotonous sawing of them with the bow.

The rhythmless cacophony seemed to act as a hypnotic on the old primitive. Head held back, eyes closed, the Indian played on, oblivious of his surroundings, and us. The discordant strain had a measure of sadness, almost as if it were reaching into the Tarahumara's mysterious, ancestral past. For me, the entire performance was a somewhat unnerving experience.

After the disturbing debut, Grandpa gave me the violin in exchange for a rat trap. The Indian realized, after a vivid demonstration, that the trap could catch small animals to supplement the family's insufficient corn diet. The loss of the treasured violin would be distressing, but not permanently so. He could make another.

It was quite late when we all retired for the night. Going to bed was no effort for the Tarahumara family. It was simply a matter of walking into the hut, and curling up on the dirt floor. Their only cover, even during the cold of winter, would be the thin clothing they wore.

Early in the morning of June 5, we bid adios to our Indian friends. We shook hands all around, hugged the children, and departed for the summit of the canyon's west wall. The Tarahumara remained silent and emotionless. We left with a lump in our throats that would take a long time to swallow.

When we reached a high and distant ridge, we stopped and looked back. Far below was the Tarahumara hut. Standing in a small knot beside it, the Indian family watched us. We waved, but they did not respond. Estelle and I looked at each other. Through the ache that filmed my eyes, I could see the tears in hers.

40

It was a trailworn and tired group that straggled into San Rafael on the evening of June 6. It was late dusk, and few people saw our return. Señor Mendez was overjoyed when we entered the station. He told us that he had expected to see us return to San Rafael after the first day of our adventure. However, after several days had elapsed, he became concerned and worried for our well-being and safety.

The night was spent in a rickety shack, adjacent to Rafael's adobe house. Jon bedded down atop a low table on the crazily slanted front stoop of our shack. Estelle and I shared a straw mattress which was lumped on an extremely narrow, springless bunk. Rough-hewn and splintery sideboards held us tightly together in rigid, cramping discomfort throughout the miserable night.

The following morning we paid Rafael and Mateo their guide fees. Both had done their tasks well, and they had taught us a great deal. We bid them a fond farewell, thanked Señor Mendez for his help, and boarded an eastbound train for Creel. We would spend a few days at the outpost Mission Sisoguichic, where we would gather more information about the Tarahumara Indians and their way of life.

CHAPTER 3

The northeastern sector
of the Tarahumara
Range is a continuation
of the geographical con-
trasts and extremes of the barranca country. Bald-
headed mountains, over nine thousand feet in

elevation, partially hide their lower nakedness under thin blankets of scrawny timber. Stern sentinels, they peer stonily into nearby deep, abysmal canyons and keep an aloof vigil over desolate plateaus and rocky mesas.

Encircled by fluted rock escarpments, barren and hopeless valleys sprawl in abject captivity. An eerie silence muffles and subdues the entire land into a dreary solitude that is broken only by the sad sigh of searching winds. The total loneliness is shattering.

Twenty-five miles southeast from the railroad village of Creel, and seventy-two hundred feet above sea level, there lies one of these valleys. Huddled on a slope of this windswept, treeless vista is the tiny Mexican settlement of Mission Sisoguichic.

Above the cluster of sun-whitened adobe buildings, a slender radio transmission tower stabs a steel finger into the sky. Nearby, a short and narrow airstrip has been laboriously gouged out of the rocky soil of the valley floor. The radio tower, and the airfield with its twin Quonset hut hangars, seem out of place in the primeval setting.

Mission Sisoguichic has more than three hundred years of turbulent, yet often dormant, history. Today, it is a growing hub of Jesuit missionary activities carried on in behalf of the Tarahumara Indians, particularly the children. The mission's facilities are necessarily crude, but they are effectively utilized.

The oldest building, of course, is the church. There is a boarding-type school that can accommodate approximately two hundred Indian children, most of them boys. A small hospital boasts an operating room, a pharmacy, a treatment clinic, and several wards totalling a sixty-bed capacity.

Woodworking and machine shops provide cabinets, tables, chairs, and the many items needed at the mission and the outlying one-room schoolhouses. There is a leather loft, where shoes, sandals, saddles, and other leather articles are made by hand. A maintenance and repair shop keeps the mission's small fleet of tired and worn jeeps and battered trucks alive and running. Electricity, strictly rationed, is provided by a simple generator powered by an ancient, single-cylinder, gasoline engine.

We arrived at Sisoguichic on June 7, 1966. The wild ride from Creel in a brakeless and dilapidated jeep was a heart-stopper. Still shivering with fright from the hair-raising journey, we met Father José A. Laguna, who insisted that we headquarter at the mission during our stay in in the area.

45

Currently the head of the mission complex, Father Laguna has been serving at Sisoguichic since 1951. An intense, dedicated, gentle, and impossibly busy man, he nevertheless always could spare the time to answer our many questions concerning the Tarahumara Indians, as well as the history of the mission.

The day before our arrival, Sisoguichic's normal peace and quiet had been shattered by violence. A half-breed Tarahumara with a penchant for trouble engaged in a shoot-out with a member of the Mexican constabulary.

The grim duel took place in the open square fronting the mission's small general store. As a knot of frightened and fascinated peasants watched, the half-breed fell to the ground, mortally wounded. Five bullets had pierced his body.

The former outlaw was placed in a hastily constructed wooden box and carted on a flatbed utility truck to a nearby slope. He was buried in a shallow pit. A small pyramid of stones marks the grave.

Shortly after the slaying in the square, another much happier event took place. "DO-CARE" (Doctors of Osteopathy Care), organized in the United States as a special project of the "Flying Osteopathic Physicians' Association," planed in to Sisoguichic.

46

Of various religious faiths, piloting their own planes at great risk, these flying doctors conduct annual mercy flights to Sisoguichic Mission hospital. This is done on their time, and at their personal expense. As a matter of interest, the bulk of the surgical instruments, hospital beds, linens, blankets, drugs, medicines, and the great quantities of supplies necessary to equip a hospital were obtained or donated by the volunteer members of DOCARE.

Except for the annual five- to ten-day visits by the American medical teams, the mission hospital has no professional medical staff available. First aid and emergency medical treatment is provided by the skilled and experienced Jesuit missionary personnel.

On rare occasions, Mexican doctors will come to Sisoguichic hospital, but only for a brief tour of duty. The remoteness and the primitive conditions surrounding the mission discourage them, and they soon return to civilization.

The American doctors direct their specialized talents toward the medical needs of the mission populace and the local peasantry. Their primary concern, however, lies with the plight of the pitiful Tarahumara Indians.

Few of the Indians will venture to the hospital for medical help. Suspicious and fearful of the white man, the Tarahumara suffers in his Stone Age ignorance, preferring the ancient and ineffectual mumbo jumbo of his own medicine men.

The several Indians who came to the hospital of their own volition were indeed pitiful cases. An emaciated nine-year-old girl reported to the doctors at the clinic, complaining of severe and lasting belly pains. A short time later I stood in the roughcast surgery and photographed the little patient as she was anesthetized by drops of ether falling on a mask.

I watched the ensuing appendectomy performed by hot, sweating experts, far removed from the comfortable, sterile perfection of their modern operating rooms in the United States.

After the operation, the patient was attended by a Jesuit sister, and an American nurse who was a member of the visiting mercy team. Three days after the operation, the stoic Tarahumara girl walked alone the fifteen miles to her cave home.

A young Indian mother of about fifteen years of age walked thirty miles to the mission hospital. Without a word, she handed her tiny, limp baby to one of the doctors. A pink froth of blood, flecked with mucous pus, barely bubbled

48

from between the infant's slightly parted lips. The diagnosis: "Pneumonia — with complications." The baby recovered.

An Indian man was brought in on a stretcher made of crossed wood sticks, borne by members of his family. Eight months previously, he had fractured his spine in an accident, and had lain helpless since. He asked the doctors to "make me walk." Since surgery might prove fatal, it was explained to the Indian that both he and his wife would have to agree to a release from responsibility.

A member of the family who was present could have taken a message to the man's wife, who had remained at home. Instead, the Tarahumara had his stretcher bearers carry him the three mile distance to his hut. Returning with his wife, they both consented to the surgery. After the operation, the man was informed that he would walk again.

A seventy-year-old Tarahumara requested that the doctors repair his crippled hands. Nine months before, the old man had fallen and broken both wrists. Unable to receive adequate medical treatment in Creel, he managed to travel the two-hundred-mile distance to Chihuahua City.

In Chihuahua, the Tarahumara was informed that nothing could be done for his condition. He returned to Creel, then went on to Sisoguichic, to await the day when the American doctors would return. The broken wristbones had long since set and healed in grotesque and immovable positions. The old Indian was unable to use either hand. To add to his misery, a severe skin disease attacked the stricken hands.

The doctors eventually came back to Sisoguichic. They explained to the Tarahumara that the skin disorder would have to be cleared up before the bones in the wrists could be rebroken, and set in their normal positions. Treatment was initiated for the skin disease. However, complete healing could not be expected before the medical team left Sisoguichic.

The operation which might restore full use of the Indian's hands was postponed. He was told to follow through on the treatment prescribed for the skin disorder, and return to the doctors on their next annual visit. The postponement did not unduly discourage the old man. He was confident and happy. Just one more year of waiting and he would, perhaps, be able to care for himself. Maybe even plant corn again!

Because of the reluctance of the Tarahumara to come to the hospital, the doctors decided to

50

take medical treatment to them. They did not have far to go. Within a thousand yards of the mission's outer limits they found Indian families living in shallow caves. Nearly every family had one or more members in dire need of medical attention.

The doctors also discovered that smallpox, typhus, tuberculosis, typhoid fever, and dysentery are the rampant killers of the Tarahumara. In addition to disease, malnutrition contributes to the unbelievably high death rate among these unfortunate peoples.

Each morning, the doctors left the hospital, eagerly looking forward to the area "cave calls" they would make that day. Each evening, they returned to the mission, frustrated and depressed at the squalor and misery they had observed. The author was informed by one of the physicians that, in three days spent among the Tarahumara, he had seen more suffering and disease than he normally would encounter during a full year's practice in one of the larger hospitals of Lansing, Michigan.

A priest and an interpreter routinely accompanied the doctors on their visits to nearby Indian dwellings. One afternoon, a doctor ventured unescorted to a hillside cave. As he approached the cave's gaping mouth, a Tarahumara man suddenly rushed out, yelling fiercely and brandishing an ugly piece of scrap iron that resembled a knife. The frightened physician ran pell-mell back to the safety of the mission. He learned a vital lesson that a visiting stranger can profit by. The shy, seemingly gentle Tarahumara can, without warning, become dangerously violent.

It was virtually impossible for us to visit an Indian family anywhere in our extensive area of travel without encountering some form of sickness among them. And all Indians, young and old, exhibit the visible results of past illnesses.

The children bear livid scars on their wan faces, particularly around the eyes and the nasal areas. Adults have their cheeks and foreheads seared and pockmarked from the ravages of past epidemics. The ever-present suppurating and infectious sores on their unwashed bodies attest to the Indians' utter ignorance of sanitation and basic hygienic measures.

Tarahumara vital statistics are startling. Two out of three babies, and many of the mothers, die at birth. Death comes from uncontrolled hemorrhage, and postnatal infection. Three out of five babies who survive the primitive birth process will succumb to disease and malnutrition before they are five years old. The survivors will rarely live to become forty-five years of age.

52

The deeper into the interior one goes from Sisoguichic, the more pitiful the Indians become. The doctors found an unconscious child, his head covered with mud and manure. The germ-laden poultice had been applied by a medicine man to cure the child's "headache." The youngster was taken to the mission hospital, where he was successfully treated for his actual illness — sleeping sickness.

Father Laguna related an incident that occurred in the autumn of 1965, when there were no doctors at the mission. One night, a group of Indians was conducting a tribal dance around a large campfire. A three-year-old Tarahumara girl stumbled, or was accidentally pushed into the fire, falling on her back across the white-hot coals.

The little girl suffered terrible burns across her shoulders, her entire back, and the backs of her legs, as far as the bend in her knees. The mother pulled the screaming child from the coals and carried her into the cave home. Except for a fanning of the seared areas, there was nothing that the mother could do for the tortured child.

Six weeks after the accident, a mission priest happened by. He discovered the small victim lying unconscious on the cold stone floor of the cave. Maggots were burrowing into the burned

53

and rotted flesh. At the mission, the girl made a complete recovery, leaving her without muscular impairment.

When we met her, she was a healthy, happy, and carefree young lady, now nearly five years old. Father Laguna is her hero, and she, in turn, is the darling-mascot of the entire mission. She will never return to her cave home. Hopefully, when she becomes an adult, the education and training received at the mission will enable her to go among her people and show them the way to a better life.

The Jesuits of Sisoguichic say that the little girl's recovery was a miracle of prayer. When the American doctors returned on their next annual visit they thoroughly examined the Tarahumara child. They tended to agree with the missionaries: her recovery had been miraculous.

A prime example of Tarahumara ignorance that results in much unnecessary physical suffering concerns their sandals, especially those worn by the younger males. The rawhide laces of these sandals are wrapped several times around the wearer's legs, just above the ankles. Once donned, the footgear is never voluntarily removed, but will remain in place until the laces are accidentally broken, or rot away from age. Before these

54

events can occur, serious complications often arise.

The uncured, tightly wrapped rawhide thongs sooner or later will become soaked from rain, or stream water. When the leather straps dry, the resultant shrinkage of the leather causes them to constrict and bite deeply into the legs, cutting off the normal circulation of blood. The entire leg, or legs, may become swollen and congested from the pressure of the dangerous tourniquets.

The sufferer will not break or cut the crippling rawhide thongs to obtain urgent relief. In his dire ignorance, he believes his problem is the work of the evil spirits, and he stoically accepts his misfortune in silent pain.

The medicine man's craft is closely associated with the evil spirits, who influence his every action. As a tribal doctor, he works diligently at his profession. In certain illnesses, he does utilize, with some measure of effectiveness, medicinal plants and herbs that grow in the deeper canyons and along the few permanent streams of the barrancas.

In general, however, the medicine man's efforts toward curing an illness or treating a severe injury are rarely successful. He is dependent upon the curative powers of his magic potions and the mumbo jumbo that he intones over his patient.

If, by chance, the patient lives through his ordeal, the medicine man receives the credit and the accolades of his associates. Should the patient die, which is the usual outcome, there is always a ready alibi: the evil spirits were too strong for the medicine man to counter.

The Tarahumara people are afraid of solar and lunar eclipses. They are convinced that sickness will come after either of these events. As a precaution, water is sprinkled over their huts or in the caves. It is believed that this will keep out the evil spirits that bring disease. The Indians follow the same procedure after witnessing a shooting star.

The spectacle of a rainbow in the sky is considered to mean certain death for whomsoever happens to look at it. The rainbow is an evil god who will eat the blood of his victim. The condemned will feel no pain.

The chile bean is highly regarded as a medicine. It is used principally in the treatment of "madness" or rabies among the Indians.

Lizards, frogs, and tadpoles are eagerly sought-after delicacies. The toad, however, is an

56

evil spirit of the first magnitude, and is avoided at all costs. It is considered poisonous, and great care is taken to store the meagre corn supply in a toad-proof place.

Should a toad hop into a dwelling and come in contact with any portion of the family's food stocks, all of the supplies must be immediately destroyed. Should this calamity occur during the cold weather months, the end result would be certain death by starvation for that unfortunate family.

The Tarahumara have a curious method of treating the bite of a rattlesnake. When an individual is bitten, attempts are made to immediately capture the snake. The rattler, called *Sayawi*, is brought to the victim, who bites deeply into the writhing reptile, just back of the head. This drastic action is supposed to neutralize the snake's evil spirits.

After these preliminary measures have been completed, the rattlesnake is penned in a small enclosure of rocks. The victim is then brought to the attention of the medicine man who applies a poultice of mud and wood ashes to the bite area. This done, everyone concerned calmly awaits the final outcome.

If the patient recovers from the bite, the medicine man decrees that the evil spirits have been

57

driven from within the snake. It is then killed, cooked, and eaten. Should the patient die, however, this indicates that the reptile's evil spirits have triumphed. The snake is then released from his prison, to slither away free and unharmed.

The unfortunate Tarahumara can never rise above their Stone Age environment until knowledge replaces abject ignorance — until truth erases degrading superstition.

The Jesuits have long recognized this great need for education among the primitive Indians. Progress toward this end has been distressingly slow. There are many valid reasons for this, not the least being the Tarahumara's inborn mistrust of all outsiders, including his benefactors.

The first step in the educational effort was the construction of a school building for the Tarahumara on the mission grounds of Sisoguichic. From its humble beginning in the early 1940's, it has grown to a facility that can accommodate approximately two hundred children. There is also a dormitory arrangement to house the Indian pupils during the annual school term, which begins in September and lasts through the following May.

In addition to the mission school, there are sixty small, log cabin schoolhouses scattered throughout the accessible parts of the Tarahumara

58

Range. Ultimate plans call for the total construction of five hundred such buildings, considered to be the minimum number for effective results from the teaching program.

The outlying schoolhouses are built with native materials, utilizing Indian labor. Each has a small classroom, equipped with a half-dozen handmade desks. A slate blackboard hangs on one wall. On a shelf near the blackboard rests a radio receiver. There are chalk, stubs of pencils, and paper tablets. Few books will be found at these schools.

One end of the building is partitioned into a separate room, which serves as the quarters for the teacher, who is usually married. (Fifty percent of the teachers manning the outpost schools are Tarahumara; many are women.)

The total cost of one school, including the furniture, school supplies, and radio receiver, is $300 (in United States currency). Sisoguichic's woodworking shops, the use of native materials, and the employment of Indian labor makes this extremely low cost possible.

The cost of teaching one pupil, per school month, is $2. The teacher's annual salary is $180, or $20 per school month. A limited amount of these expenses is met by the Mexican government, which only recently recognized the Tarahumara Indians as wards of the state.

Since the government maintains a strict "hands off" policy on religious matters, the Jesuits must comply with very specific and restrictive regulations to receive financial assistance. The funds are earmarked for Tarahumara educational use, and must not be expended for other purposes.

To supplement the government grant of $250 (U.S.) per month, the Jesuits accept cash and material donations submitted by private sources on both sides of the Mexico-United States border.

Enrollment in the Tarahumara schools is on a voluntary basis. The pupils range in age from six to fourteen years, and the grades extend from the first through the fourth. The average enrollment at Mission Sisoguichic school is eighty pupils. The outlying district schools will average four to six children per school term.

The great majority of children attending school are boys. Unless the family lives quite near the school, a girl seldom is enrolled. Tarahumara children must obtain parental consent to attend the school at the mission and live at the dormitory. This permission is always readily granted. With a child off to school for nine months, there is one less mouth to feed — one more chance to fend off a winter of possible starvation.

Father Arroyo, director of education at Sisoguichic, said that the Indian pupils apparently do not miss their family ties while at school, but rather seem quite happy. School, to them, means trading their loincloths for denim trousers, having warm beds to sleep in, and most important enjoying the secure feeling that a full stomach can generate.

When the school term ends in the spring, the children return to their families. The mission fathers will transport them to their homes by jeep, where that is possible. Some are flown to the areas of their homes by Father Laguna. The majority of the youngsters walk to their family dwellings, some of which are located sixty miles or more from Sisoguichic.

Tarahumara boys like everything about school, except the necessary studying. If the teachers apply pressure upon them in order to improve their study habits, they sulk, frequently leaving school, never to return. The general lack of motivation is attributed to the Indians' low IQ. This, in turn, may be partially blamed upon the brain-damaging results of prolonged malnutrition.

The work load of the pupils is actually very light. Basic Spanish, reading, and writing are the principal subjects. Elementary personal hygiene is taught. There is also a brief course on the known Tarahumara history and culture.

Nearly all of the Tarahumara who have attended school at Mission Sisoguichic will readily proclaim that they are Christians. However, upon return to their respective families, what they have learned about Christianity is not practiced and is soon forgotten. The primitive Tarahumara are much more comfortable wearing the ancient mantle of tribal superstitions bestowed upon them by their fathers.

Very few of the Indian children complete the fourth grade of school. Those who finish the course receive certificates of graduation. These are taken home where they are lost or destroyed. The parents show no interest in a child's scholastic efforts or achievements.

There have been some of the Tarahumara who have filtered out of the barrancas and extended their education at elementary schools in Chihuahua City, and even as far away as Monterrey. There is no record of a Tarahumara ever having enrolled in a college or university.

The Jesuits have developed a novel teaching method for use in the outlying schools. The daily lessons are broadcast from the low-wattage radio transmitter at Sisoguichic. At the outpost schools, the teachers receive the instructions through the receiver installed in the classroom. The lessons are transferred to the blackboard, thence to the pupils.

The mission station beams only Spanish language lessons, health information, and important weather news to the schools. Mexican law prohibits the dissemination of religious doctrine over the airwaves.

During the vacation months, the majority of the male teachers gather at Sisoguichic for further training and study. In addition to attending "summer school," they work in the various mission shops, drive trucks, help in road construction, and are employed in other activities of the mission complex.

It was near the end of June, and time for us to return home. We had traveled far and wide in the unbelievable Tarahumara barranca country. We had learned much about its primitive peoples — but not enough. Even as we wended our way home we made plans to return at the earliest opportunity.

CHAPTER 4

In the late spring of 1967, we again returned to the land of the Tara-humara. This time, we would backpack deep into the interior, set up a base camp, and live among the primitive Indians.

65

We first went to Sisoguichic and asked Father Laguna where we might find a representative number of Tarahumara Indians living in an accessible region of the interior. He recommended the area of Tehuerichic, located along the headwaters of Río Conchos, approximately sixty miles southeast of Sisoguichic.

Remembering the great communication problem we had with the Tarahumara on our previous contacts, we borrowed an interpreter from the mission, a lean, friendly Mexican known as "Eppie."

Born at the mission, Eppie was well versed in the Tarahumara language. His limited knowledge of English had been learned in Texas, where he had spent several uneasy years as a "wetback," the term given a Mexican national who wades or swims across the Rio Grande to avoid the red tape for legal entry into the United States.

The first leg of our journey into the interior was by jeep to Panaluchic, a tiny mission outpost perhaps thirty miles from Sisoguichic. We continued a few miles beyond Panaluchic, where the terrain became impassable for the jeep. Reminding the driver that he was to meet us at that point two weeks hence, we bid him adios, and hoisted our packs. After the battering we had endured in the jeep, it was a pleasure to strike out on foot.

66

Shortly after we began walking, we met a young Tarahumara whom we had met and photographed at Sisoguichic the previous year. He recognized us immediately and greeted us warmly with the unique Tarahumara finger-to-palm handshake. He was en route to the small store at Panaluchic to barter for corn and cloth.

Later, we came upon an Indian lad who was perhaps ten years of age. He was plowing a small parcel of shalelike land, preparing it for corn planting. The crude wooden plow that he steered so skillfully was unusual in that there was not a bit of metal in its construction.

The plowshare was the pointed end of a small log, which was about two feet in length and eight inches in diameter. The depth of the furrow that trickled behind it was about two inches in depth. The handle consisted of a single long pole driven into a slot that had been carved into the log.

Motive power for the plow was supplied by two lanky, plodding oxen. The team was yoked to a pole that served as the plow tongue. The yoke was a length of rough-carved wooden beam, tapered on both ends, and lying across the top of the animals' broad heads. It was secured to the bases of their long, sweeping horns by wide strips of weathered rawhide.

I expressed my desire to try my hand at the

67

plow. The boy readily handed me the single rawhide rein, and a slender willow whip. I flicked the near ox with the tip of the switch, and the oxen, plow, and I lumbered across the rough and rocky field.

I tried in vain to control the careening plow and the confused, meandering beasts. I was indeed happy when the young Indian relieved me of the rein and the whip and effortlessly brought the oxen-plow combination back on a straight course. My family's and Eppie's loud guffaws did little for my acute discomfiture.

Occasionally, we saw small herds of goats clinging to the steep and barren higher slopes. The goats were always tended by Tarahumara women, each of whom usually had a baby strapped to her back with a wide swath of cloth. We were never able to meet these women, as they would scurry out of sight at our approach.

There were few Indian men in evidence on our trip to Tehuerichic. Those whom we chanced to meet on the trail gave us wide berth, watching us with unfeigned suspicion and hostility.

Eppie had never before ventured so far into the interior of the barranca country. When the Indians ignored his greetings, and answered him instead with ugly scowls, he became visibly upset. His ready smile disappeared, he seldom

68

spoke, and his sharp, black eyes nervously probed the surrounding terrain, as if he expected an ambush.

The only time that danger threatened us was prompted by my incurable curiosity. It was late evening, and we were looking for a campsite. Suddenly, from up ahead, came the strident wail of a violin. The discordant rendition was grating from the interior of a rock hut squatted on a slope. Outside, leaning against a corner of the hovel, stood an Indian woman. She was watching us.

We left the trail and began climbing the slope. An old Tarahumara man came from behind the hut, rapidly fiddling a handmade violin. We stopped in front of the couple and Eppie greeted them in their native tongue. The slatternly woman ignored the greeting and remained silent. The gnarled old fiddler continued playing his raucous discord. He stared hard at Eppie and me, glanced briefly at Estelle and Jon, then turned and said something to the woman.

She entered the hut, and almost immediately two Indian men came out, their faces contorted into ugly grimaces. As they advanced menacingly toward us, I ordered my family and Eppie to walk, not run, back to the trail, and wait for me.

Moving backwards a few feet I stopped, alert to every movement of the slowly oncoming

Indians. Neither of them had a knife or other visible weapon. I fitted an arrow in the crossbow and held my ground. When the primitives were within ten feet of me, I raised the bow and aimed directly at the belly of the nearest Indian. They both understood. Quick fear replaced the fierce scowls, and the two men retreated to the hut.

Throughout the entire incident, the old Tarahumara had not ceased playing his violin. I rejoined my group on the trail, and we wasted no time in putting as much distance as possible between us and the Indians. Long after the hut was out of sight, we could still hear the rasping serenade of the wild troubador.

The scenery on the way to Tehuerichic is beautiful and ever changing. We held our route mainly to dry waterways and boulder-strewn valleys. The stream beds often led us between precipitous canyon walls. The valleys, not as immediately confining, were flanked by parallel rocky escarpments of great heights. The strange palisades seemed to serve as giant pedestals for the forested mountain slopes, which, in turn, gave way to towering rocky peaks.

After the extreme heat and the physical hardships we had suffered on our exploration of Barranca Urique, the journey to Tehuerichic was a distinct pleasure. The sun was pleasantly warm, and the mild breezes were invigorating. At elevations of seven thousand to eight thousand feet the nights were nippy, but we were snug in our small tent. Eppie, wrapped in a woolen serape, slept on the ground beside a wood fire.

We arrived at Tehuerichic the second day out of Sisoguichic. Located on a shelf-land facing the serpentine Río Conchos, it consisted of two newly constructed buildings — a small church, and a one-room schoolhouse with an earthen floor.

A short distance from the church stood the more than three-hundred-year-old adobe and rock ruins of the original Jesuit mission. On a nearby slope, a crumbling rock wall encircled the old mission cemetery, where disarranged heaps of greying stones marked the gravesites of pioneer men of the cloth who had given their lives for a conviction.

The only residents of Tehuerichic were preparing to leave. The school was closed for the summer period, and the teacher, a twenty-six-year-old Tarahumara with the Christian name of Reyes Guadalupe, his wife, and their five-year-old son would walk to Sisoguichic. At the central mission, Mr. Guadalupe would work and also attend summer school. He would return to Tehuerichic with his family in time to begin the next school term in September.

At Father Laguna's insistence, we had agreed

71

to use a small annex of the church as our head-
quarters during our stay in the area. Reyes, as he
preferred to be called, gave us the keys to the
annex, and also the keys to the schoolroom, where
Eppie would be quartered.

Our first order of business was to find the
local leader, or chief, of the Tarahumara, and,
hopefully, make his acquaintance. His friendship
and cooperation was of the utmost importance if
we were to obtain firsthand and reliable information on the Indians' way of life.

Reyes postponed his departure for Sisoguichic
one full day, explaining that he knew the chief
well, and that he might be of assistance to us in
the initial phases of our meeting with the leader.
Depositing our packs in the church annex, we
followed Reyes down the slope that led to the
river. It was the annual dry season, and the Río
Conchos was at low ebb. We easily waded across
to the high ground that extended beyond.

Less than a mile from Tehuerichic, we came
to the split-log lean-to dwelling of the chief. He
was standing outside, watching our approach.
About forty years of age, slender and sinewy, the
chief was dressed in the loose shirt and loincloth
common to all Tarahumara males. The very thin,
slightly bowed, and naked legs made him appear
taller than his five and one-half feet. A red cloth
headband encircled his jet black hair, and he wore

72

the commonplace sandals with rawhide lacings.

The simple formalities of our awkward meeting were handled by the schoolteacher. The chief, whose name was Borrijic, completely ignored Eppie. His piercing black eyes flicked over me and my family, then dismissed us as of no immediate interest. It was evident to us that the introductions were finished.

Our meeting ended in keen disappointment. We had not made a favorable impression, nor had we received even a hint that the taciturn chieftain would cooperate with us in our projected study of his people.

On our way back to Tehuerichic, I asked Reyes why Chief Borrijic had been so brusque and unfriendly. Reyes said that the chief had actually been well impressed with us, and that we could expect a visit from him the next morning.

Shortly after sunrise on the following morning, Chief Borrijic appeared in the open doorway of the annex. I had just completed the preparation of breakfast, and invited him to join us. Wordlessly, he turned on his heel and walked swiftly to the schoolhouse, where Reyes and his family were stirring about.

We finished our breakfast and stepped outside. The chief and Reyes immediately joined us. Chief Borrijic smiled broadly and extended the fingers of his right hand, caressing my palm with the tips. We were friends!

The chief agreed to help us in our quest for information about his people. He volunteered to escort us to any part of his wide district that we might want to visit. Furthermore, he would intercede for us with such Indian families or individuals we might observe and question. Chief Borrijic also accepted Eppie as an interpreter, although he did not stroke his palm in friendship.

I thanked Reyes for his part in bringing the reluctant chief and us together. Embarrassed, the teacher quickly disclaimed any credit, saying that if Chief Borrijic had not wanted to cooperate with us, no one could have changed his mind. Reyes then called his family to him, bade us farewell, and left for Sisoguichic. We would miss this intelligent, friendly, and helpful Tarahumara.

Although wards of the state, the Tarahumara tribe remains self-governed. There being precious little to arbitrate or administrate, the political realm is enviably pure, and simple.

Politically, the land is divided into several districts, each with an elected leader, or chief. Presiding over the combined districts is a governor, who acts as the final judge in matters beyond the scope or ken of the local chieftains. Selection of the leaders is by popular consent of the people, rather than by ballot.

74

The three-year term of office is largely symbolic, as the incumbents usually remain in office until voluntary resignation, retirement, or death. There being no monetary system among the Tarahumara, leaders serve without pay.

Qualifications for office are largely based on personality and a thorough knowledge of tribal traditions. Being a witch doctor or a medicine man, or having a good working knowledge of their crafts, also carries a great deal of influence. Some of the chiefs are selected because of their proven ability to win a *rarahipa*, or kickball race. Economical status of the nominee plays no part in the election. The chiefs are as destitute and hungry as their constituents.

The principal functions of the chief seem to be the settling of occasional family or individual disputes, and the holding of a one-man court of law for the trial of the infrequent offender of the established social order.

The Indians respect the authority of their chosen chief. However, the real power and influence rests with the witch doctors, who perpetuate the ancient tribal tenets that are steeped in fear and superstition. The dire penalties that may be imposed by the witch doctors are more to be feared than the relatively mild punishments meted offenders by the elected officials.

Crime, as we know it, is almost nonexistent

among the primitive Indians. This may be due, in large measure, to the fact that the Tarahumara live in widely scattered groups of two or three families. If they were crowded into a communal environment, the attendant human pressures would soon spawn the seeds of discontent and mischief.

Thievery is rare. This was demonstrated to us each time we made an extended field trip away from our base. Wanting to travel light, we would leave the bulk of our supplies, including food stocks, behind. On our return, everything would be exactly as we had left it. Chief Borrijic told me that I could leave a sack of corn (the most valuable item of the Tarahumara possessions) in the open, unattended, for days on end, and the Indians would not touch it.

We asked the chief to comment on the offenses most frequently committed by the Indians living within the scope of his jurisdiction. After prolonged thought, he indicated that sometimes a quarrel between two Indians would erupt into personal combat.

Scuffling and wrestling are the usual methods of fighting. Fists are not used. In the more serious altercations the combatants will resort to beating each other with rocks and clubs.

Chief Borrijic explained that the fights normally occur during a social gathering, when the *teshuino* (a native corn liquor) is flowing freely. At these functions, the chief is often compelled to warn the participants against becoming too noisy and excited.

Justice for the Tarahumara is swift and simple in application. After an open trial, the guilty party, or parties, is sentenced by the chief to a period of hard labor. The sentence is executed under the supervision of the person seeking redress.

In the rare case of murder, the guilty Indian is brought by the chief before the Tarahumara governor. The governor imposes the standard penalty of imprisonment at hard labor for a period of five years. The convicted man is escorted to the Chihuahua City prison, where he serves his sentence. For the freedom-loving Tarahumara, five years behind prison walls is tantamount to a sentence of death.

Chief Borrijic had been chosen as chief three weeks prior to our coming to Tehuerichic. His predecessor had voluntarily resigned at the unusual Tarahumara age of sixty-two years. Inquiry revealed that the former chief lived in a cave about six miles from Tehuerichic. Chief Borrijic agreed to guide us to the old man's home.

The cave was situated on the ledge of a cliff overlooking the Río Conchos. The ex-chief was not at home, but we took the liberty of examining

77

and photographing his cave dwelling. The interior was typically barren of possessions — a metate, several gourd bowls, and a few scattered corncobs. At one side of the cave was a thin layer of dried grass and leaves. This was the bed.

We descended the cliff and found the old man on the bank of the river. He was lying on the ground, with his head cradled on the rotting trunk of a fallen cottonwood tree. Ignoring our greetings, he arose and muttered a few words to Borrijic. The two men moved away from us and walked out of sight around a bend in the river.

An hour later, Chief Borrijic returned alone. He said that the old man had gone upriver, and that he would not return that day. Our hopes dashed for an interesting interview, we returned to Tehuerichic.

Several days later, the old man, accompanied by Borrijic, paid us a surprise visit. His hostility had softened, but he would not converse with us. We were amazed when Chief Borrijic told us that the old fellow had walked the rugged six miles from his cave to Tehuerichic in slightly less than two hours. The same route had taken us nearly four hours to accomplish.

During the first days with the chief, we held to the formalities and always addressed him as "Chief Borrijic." From the beginning he called us by our first names. We soon followed suit, and nicknamed him "Pat," an appellation that always brought a wide, toothy grin to his wrinkled, leathery face.

Pat was a man of strong, swiftly changing moods. We never really knew how to approach him. At one moment he would be deeply interested in a discussion, eagerly answering our questions. In the midst of a phrase, he would suddenly lapse into a morose, tight-lipped silence, seemingly resentful of our very presence.

When he was in one of his sullen moods, we left him completely alone. In a short time, he would come to us like a penitent child, grinning his way back into our good graces.

The chief never once expressed a curiosity about us, nor the land from whence we had come. We volunteered pertinent information about the United States and our modern way of living. However, Pat could not comprehend a life so completely different from his own.

The single topic that sparked a response from the chief concerned food. This subject he could understand. When I told him that relatively few of my countrymen suffered the pangs of hunger, the chief replied that all Tarahumara suffer from lack of sufficient food from the day of birth, and remain hungry until the day of death.

Pat admired my long-bladed and heavy Bowie knife; however, the crossbow was the main item of our equipment that caught his lasting fancy. I gave him a shooting demonstration, and thereafter he insisted on carrying the bow and the quiver of arrows wherever we went. Being allowed to carry the weapon gave him a distinct badge of importance among his fellows, and also indicated that he held a special mark of trust.

From the first to the last of our many field trips together, Pat wordlessly let it be known to us that he was in command. I held my family to a strict ruling that when on the trail, we would take a ten-minute rest break every hour. Chief Pat looked upon these interludes with great disfavor. While we rested, he would squat on his heels, impatient to move on. After a few moments of waiting he would arise and brusquely command *"Mashi-mabu!"* This means "Let's go!" Without a backward glance, Pat would stride down the trail. We had to run to catch up with him.

A journey with the chief was always difficult. He never led us by the easiest, nor the most direct, route to our objective. Often we arrived at our destination almost too exhausted to cover our assigned mission.

Except for Pat's refusual to join us at breakfast on the morning he had agreed to cooperate with us and help us obtain information, he never

80

refused an invitation to share a meal with us. Always hungry, he would smack his appreciation of our food to the last morsel. It was gnawing hunger that caused the chief to lead us on the innumerable detours from our planned courses.

As he walked ahead of us, Pat constantly searched the ground, scanned the bushes and trees, and peered under rocks, looking for anything that might be edible. Small matter whether the occasional tidbit he discovered or captured was a sluggish and slimy grub, a hairy worm, or a fat-legged grasshopper — he popped it into his mouth with obvious relish.

The chief once halted us and had us wait while he climbed a tree and robbed a bird's nest of three tiny fledglings. Methodically, he pinched the birds' heads between two fingers, and quickly plucked the scrawny growth of fuzzy feathers. The diminutive raw morsels sustained Pat until later in the day, when he knocked a bird from a tall tree with one well-aimed rock.

Hitting the bird from a distance of at least thirty feet was no mere coincidence. From early childhood, the Tarahumara males practice throwing rocks at real and fancied targets. By the time they reach maturity, killing small game by this primitive method will have become routine.

The majority of the Indians of the Tehuerichic area reside along, or near, the Río Conchos. The high cliffs and steep slopes that contain the twisting river are pockmarked with natural caves — the winter homes of the Tarahumara.

In early spring, the Indian families will descend from the caves and live in lean-to shelters erected on benchlands and hills well above the river's high water level. The summer homes are located close to the numerous sweeping bends of the Río Conchos, where the annual rainy season floods have deposited layers of silt and sandy soil.

The Indians plant their corn in the silt and sand. The small plots are planted and tended in a manner centuries removed from modern methods of cultivation. Instead of a plow pulled by a tractor, the Tarahumara breaks the soil by hand with a pointed stick. A very few of them are more fortunate — the pointed stick is pulled by one, or perhaps two, oxen. Instead of using a steel hoe, the Tarahumara scratches at the weeds with the same stick.

Because the Indian knows nothing about irrigation, the life-sustaining corn droops from a killing thirst, only a few feet away from the flowing river. Some of the corn will, in spite of conditions, mature and ripen. Most of it will be washed away by the rising waters of the rainy season.

During our short stay at Tehuerichic, we visited more than twenty families. Trying to learn of the habits and customs of the Tarahumara family units was one of our greatest frustrations. We found the women apathetic, unconcerned, and uncooperative. They were usually afraid of us, and sometimes hostile — particularly if their husbands were absent.

The inability of the women to give us information may have been due to an utter lack of comprehension. Interrogation through an interpreter can be a difficult process, even when practiced between civilized peoples.

The information we were able to gather concerning the Indians' family life was gained generally through close observation of the chief's family, with whom we were most closely associated.

Chief Pat and his wife had a fifteen-year-old married daughter and three sons. One boy was three years of age, the next eighteen months, and the youngest an infant of six weeks. The twelve-year span between the daughter and the eldest son represented a void left by five additional children who had perished from disease and/or malnutrition.

The daughter, her sixteen-year-old husband, and their two young children lived with her parents. Thus, nine persons were crowded into

83

a lean-to shelter of poles and upright logs that boasted a floor space of less than 110 square feet.

The daily routine of the chief's household was the same as that of the other Indian families. The women and older girls bestir themselves at dawn's first light, kindling the still smoldering wood coals of yesterday's fire. The corn for the cakes having been metated and shaped the evening before, preparation of breakfast is simply a matter of tossing several corn cakes on the hot rocks lying loosely in the open fire.

In a manner of speaking, breakfast is served to the members of the family while they are still in bed. Sluggishly awakening from their huddled positions on the dusty dirt floor, and sitting cross-legged, they patiently wait for their helpings of corn cakes to be handed to them.

The Indian women and the girls who are old enough to help are always busy. There is water to be carried from the river for family use. This entails a trip of at least a half mile from home. While at the river, the women may launder individual items of clothing they happen to be wearing. The washing chore is simple, but effective.

After wetting the article in the river water, it is placed on a large flat stone. The encrusted dirt is beaten from the cloth by means of a rock held in the hand. The clothing is sloshed in the river and is spread over a bush to dry. If no bush is available, a large boulder serves the purpose.

Work in the cornfield is generally the women's task. The men and boys will help in the field when not engaged in hunting, fishing, or visiting with other Indians.

Sometimes, the metate used to grind corn, becomes badly cracked or broken. The lot of making a new metate falls to the women. The first step in the operation is the selection of a stone of the proper type and size. Using a pointed flint rock as a tool, the women laboriously chip the stone into an oblong shape. The top of the metate is then troughed and slanted toward one end.

The entire procedure is a slow and tedious chore, requiring many long hours of patient chipping to complete. The flint rock is also used as the tool to form a stone into the size and shape of a brick. This stone is pushed and pulled across the troughed surface of the metate, cracking the corn into a coarse meal.

The children who are not old enough to assist in the work are left to their own devices. We saw no evidence of toys, games, or anything resembling a doll. Nor did we see any of the Indian youngsters running or chasing each other in play. They would sit mutely near the elders, or would lie asleep on the hard ground, the matter weeping from their noses oozing down the sides of their cheeks.

The babies are usually left inside the shelter, where they spend most of the time asleep. Strangely, we never heard a Tarahumara infant cry — including the many who were suffering from illness or hunger. Conversely, we rarely heard the children laugh. Happiness is indeed a stranger in the land of the Tarahumara.

When an Indian mother leaves her home in pursuit of a task, her baby is carried on her back, the infant slumped contentedly in the restraining folds of a wide cloth band.

C H A P T E R 5

Nearly all of the Indian families we visited owned one or more dogs. The animals showed no excitement or concern at our intrusions, not bothering to issue so much as a bark or growl of warning.

87

Questionable as to breed, the dogs are small and gaunt: the outlines of their ribs are plainly visible beneath the taut hides. The mongrels serve no apparent useful purpose. They rarely accompany their masters on the frequent hunts, or travels, but remain listlessly at the Indians' dwellings.

The Tarahumara cannot regularly feed the dogs, and there are seldom any leftovers from a meal to toss them. The starved animals become sly and expert thieves, snatching scraps of corn cake from the unwary eaters, especially the children.

The dogs are not petted or otherwise fondled by the Indians. Neither are they mistreated, except for an occasional swift kick. At night, if space can be found on the crowded floor, the animals sleep with the family.

Knowing nothing of sanitation, the Tarahumara do not, of course, have toilets, or outdoor privies. Body wastes are deposited on the ground a short distance from the dwellings. From personal observation, I would suggest that the dogs depend upon these wastes to keep alive.

We saw no puppies or young dogs. Most of the animals I saw were female. Considering the plight of the Tarahumara, it is very possible that dog meat is an essential part of the Indians' sparse diet.

88

I was vitally interested in learning from Chief Pat as much as I could of the origin of his tribe, and how long the Tarahumara had lived in the terrible canyon country. He could tell me very little.

According to their legends, the Tarahumara originally "came down from the sky with corn in their ears." We examined the caves, searching for artifacts, hieroglyphics, or other clues that might shed light on this people's past history. We found nothing.

We had heard at Sisoguichic, and also at Creel, that the Apache Indians once lived in the land of the Tarahumara. Chief Pat insisted that the stories were true. Like the Tarahumara, the Apache had lived in the caves. Unlike the Tarahumara, he had been a fierce warrior, constantly on the warpath — many times, against his neighbor the Tarahumara.

Legend has it that the Apache departed the barranca country perhaps seven hundred years ago. The Tarahumara do not know where the feared warriors went. According to tradition, the Apaches maintained annual pilgrimages to their former cave homes until times of recent history.

(It is an established fact that the Apaches made extended journeys into Mexico from the areas of what are now West Texas, New Mexico, and Arizona. A portion of the ancient trail still leads through the Chisos Mountains of Big Bend National Park. The route crossed the Rio Grande and extended into the mountains south of the river. The theory has been advanced that the Apache made this annual trek to the mountains in Mexico to hunt more-abundant game. Perhaps the old trail is indeed the pilgrimage route that led the dreaded Apache back to his ancestral home — the caves of the Tarahumara Range.)

Chief Pat escorted Jon and me to the vicinity of a cave which he said was once inhabited by Apaches. About five miles from Tehuerichic, and facing the Río Conchos, the cave was far removed from those inhabited by the Tarahumara.

We asked Pat to accompany us to the cave, but he refused, preferring to wait for us near the river. According to the chief, a cave suspected to have been the home of Apaches is avoided by the Tarahumara.

We found no markings or drawings on the walls of the cave. Jon located a pear-shaped stone that resembled an axe or tomahawk head. It was partially buried in the dust of centuries on the rock floor. We failed to sift arrows, spear points, or other artifacts from the dust and debris. We emerged from the cave and rejoined the chief at the river. He was obviously relieved to see us again and anxious to return to Tehuerichic.

90

The language of the Tarahumara remains generally unadulterated, notwithstanding the many years of exposure to the Spanish-speaking missionaries and other foreign influences. Unlike the guttural tones of many aboriginal tongues, the Tarahumara words are fluid and musical in sound. Many of them have what seems to be a Polynesian flavor.

Chief Pat was pleased that I wanted to learn as much of his language as time, and my limited ability, permitted. With his cooperation, and the help of Eppie's interpretive chores, I enrolled in a part-time language course.

The sessions were conducted whenever the chief was in a teaching mood. School was held daily — on the open trail, in musty caves, by the campfire at the chief's dwelling, and at our base camp.

Generally, the chief was a patient teacher. He possessed a keen sense of humor, frequently laughing outright at my stumbling confusion. There were times, however, when he became annoyed at my struggles with a certain word. By his emphatic growls of displeasure, and his frantic arm-waving, I meekly gathered that I was considered to be a rather dense pupil.

Since the Tarahumara do not write, the language lessons were presented orally. Through Eppie, I would ask Chief Pat the Tarahumara equivalent of a particular English word or phrase. I would repeat this translation over and over, until he was satisfied with my pronunciation. Only then would Pat permit me to advance to the next word or term.

The Tarahumara words and expressions in the following short glossary are presented phonetically, followed by the English translation.

ABU-WAY: Stop
A-TA-KAW WA-KAW: Bow and Arrow

BA-CO-CHEE: River
BA-TOO-KEE: Raccoon
BOW-A-KA: Sheep
BOW-A-SICK-EE: Wool
BO-WEE-KEE: Trail

CHEE-BA: Goat
CHEE-MA-DRAY-WAY: Name
CHO-MA-LICK-EE: Deer
CHOO-ROO-KIKI: Bird

DOO-LA-WA: Cold
DRAW-LA-MOO-DEE: Indian
DRAW-YAWN-A-LEE: Sun
DRAY-MECK-EE: Corn Cake
DRAY-SO-CHICK-EE: Cave
DRAY-TOO-KOO: Ice
DRO-KAW: Night

92

EE-KAW-KAW: Wind
EP-EE RA-WAY SA-BA-DU:
  This is the sixth day.

GA-RA-HOO-KOO: That is right.
GAW-NEE-REE: Happy
GAW-RAY-RU-A-MEE: (Term of
  Affection)
GAW-REE-MA: Love
GAW-OO: Horse
GEE-MA-KA: Blanket
GO-CHEE-ME-A: Sleep
GOOK: Firewood
GOO-CHOO-KOO: Dried Fish
GOO-NA: Husband

KA-A-WICK-EE: Mountains
KA-WAD-DA: Bird Egg
KAW-PA-RICK-EE: Snow
KEE-OO-MER-O: I cannot.
KO-CHICK-EE: Dog
KOR-A-GAW-KA: Beads
KOR-EEMA-KA-WONE: Soap

MA-BU SA-DEE: Let's eat.
MA-CHONA-BA: (A Greeting)
MA-LA: Daughter
MA-NA-DICK-EE: Fish Trap
MA-POLA KOW-ERA: Headband
MA-SEE-MEE: Walking

MA-SHEE MA-BU: Let's go.
MAY-SAW-KA: Moon
MA-YAW: Puma
MOO-CHEE: Children
MO-HEH: You
MOO-KEE-KEE: Girl
MOO-NICK-EE: Beans
MOO-SA: Wildcat

NA-NA: Mother
NO-LA: Son
NO-LICK-EE: Clouds
NEY-HEY: Me
NEY-HEY BA-WICKI BA-HEE-MA:
 Me drink water.
NEY-HEY NEE-WA LA-HOO-COO:
 Mine (Possessive Pronoun)

O-NO: Father
OO-KOO-MEE-A: Rain
OOP-EE: Wife
OO-REE: Yes

QWEE-RA-BA: (A Greeting)

RA-CHICK-EE: Fish
RA-RA-HEEPA: Kickball Race
RO-WICK-EE: Rabbit

SAY-KO-LICK-EE: Earthen Pot
SA-YAW-WEE: Rattlesnake

94

SEP-O-LICK-EE: Stars
SEP-O-LICK-EE WEE-TISH-MA:
Falling Star
SOO-NOO-COO: Corn

TOW-ICK-EE: Boy
TOW-NA-REE: Feast
TU-TU-GOO-REE: Owl

WA-EE-DICK-EE: Basket

YU-MA-REE: Dance

It is of interest to note that the Tarahumara have no words for directions, i.e., north, south, east, or west. They have no need for them, as they know their country as well as we do our own backyards.

There are many species of birds and animals in the barranca country. Game may be abundant in some of the more secluded areas of the deep interior, but in the regions we traveled it is far from plentiful. This may be due to the combined factors of rigorous environment and the constant foraging of the hungry Tarahumara.

Nearly all forms of wildlife are hunted for food. The seldom seen bear is never molested by the Indians, who believe that the spirits of their ancestors reside within the body of the beast.

95

The Indians' methods of killing or capturing animals are of course extremely primitive. The crude longbows are quite powerful, but the wood-tipped arrows are warped, and inaccurate, except at close range. This weapon is used mainly to kill small animals and the larger birds and wildfowl.

The Tarahumara kill deer with the bow and arrow, but they prefer to run the animal down. In its final stages of helpless exhaustion, the deer is killed by a blow on the head with a rock.

Sportsmen well know the crafty ability of the wild turkey to evade his hunters. Yet the fleet-footed and enduring Tarahumara literally runs the bird to death. Forced into a rapid series of takeoffs, without sufficient rest periods between, the heavy-bodied bird does not have the strength to fly or run from a bare-handed capture by its relentless pursuer.

The Indians use a simple trigger-trap to capture game. Selecting a site with a stone surface, or base, a flat rock is placed on edge at about a forty-five degree angle. The rock slab is supported in this position by an upright stick of wood. One end of a smaller piece of wood is cleverly tied by a length of rawhide, or strands of yucca fibre, to the base of the support stick, and thus becomes the trap trigger.

At the opposite end of the trigger stick,

which extends well beneath the tilted rock slab, is fastened a piece of meat or other form of bait. When an animal goes beneath the slab and tugs at the bait, the trigger stick releases the main support, bringing the heavy, overhanging rock down upon the animal and crushing it to death.

There is no danger of the game being eaten by other animals before the owner of the trap returns. Except for the protruding hind legs and the tail, the rest of the prize is securely pinned between the stone base, and the trap's rock slab, and cannot be dug out.

The use of the rock trap is not confined to small game. It is also set to capture and kill larger beasts, such as the powerful puma, or mountain lion. The trap's mechanics are simple — the bigger the animal to be trapped, the larger the rock must be that falls upon it.

The Tarahumara uses another means to capture deer besides running the animal down or shooting it with an arrow. In its normal habits, a deer regularly follows a main run, or trail, in its travels between the feeding grounds and the nearest stream or water hole. Somewhere along the rough and uneven route, the deer must leap from a small ledge or precipice that intersects the trail. At the bottom of such a barrier, the wily Tarahumara places sharpened sticks, or slender poles, in an upright position, anchoring them

97

by propping stones against the bases. As the deer progresses down the trail, an Indian will suddenly dart from a hidden position and give chase. Frightened, and traveling at great speed, the hapless animal approaches the ledge, leaps forward and down, and impales itself upon the pointed sticks below.

The Indians have two principal methods of catching fish. The first consists of a net, or trap, made of reeds. The reeds, which grow along the banks of the larger streams, are each about a half-inch in diameter and are cut in approximately three-foot lengths. These are tied parallel to each other by means of fibre strands of the yucca plant. The finished net looks like a long section of picket fence. The net is spread across a narrow portion of the stream to be fished. Each end of the net is held by an Indian. Other men of the fishing party move upstream and throw large rocks into the water. In the resultant commotion, the startled fish rush downstream, where they collide with the net and are promptly hauled ashore.

We accompanied the chief on one of these fishing trips. The catch was a good one, consisting of eighteen perchlike fish, averaging five inches in length. The Indians divided the catch, each receiving an equal share.

Chief Pat took his fish home, where he split

them in two with his fingers. He placed the connected halves of fish on top of a flat rock. I supposed that the fish were to be dried, and perhaps stored for later use. At the end of the second day, the chief and his family enjoyed a supper of sun-baked, well-putrefied fish.

In the second method of fishing, the Tarahumara utilize the leaves of a peculiar plant that grows in the deep canyons. The leaves are shredded into small bits and tossed into a quiet area of the stream to be fished. In a surprisingly short time, the built-in toxic qualities of the leaves stun the fish into a bellies-up immobility.

The fisherman has only to wade out in the water and pick up his catch. The knocked-out fish which may be overlooked by the harvesting fisherman will soon regain their equilibrium and swim away, none the worse for the experience. The Indians suffer no apparent ill effect from eating the drugged fish.

Chief Pat led us to a high, razor-backed ridge overlooking the river to a lookout point reportedly used by the Apache. We found only the crumbled remains of what had been a rock-walled hut.

As we stood by the ruins, Jon pointed to a cloud of blue-black smoke billowing upward from a distant ridge beyond the Río Conchos. The rocky terrain, sparsely covered with scrub oak and thin underbrush, presented little danger of a spreading fire.

The chief explained that a witch doctor had started the blaze, in the belief that it would bring rain. This superstitious custom has been practiced by the Tarahumara for centuries. The fires have resulted in the destruction of vast forest lands and the elimination of much natural cover for vital game.

The fires have also caused the deaths of Indian families who became hopelessly trapped in the consuming fury of unchecked flames.

The Tarahumaras' only alcoholic beverage is called teshuino, and is fermented from the green shoot, or sprout, of the corn plant. Teshuino drinking is reserved for ceremonial occasions, and for the infrequent social gatherings enjoyed by the Indians. Drunkenness is rare, since they can ill afford to divert much of the precious corn-producing plant to the manufacture of teshuino.

Chief Pat arranged a teshuino party, at which we were to be the guests of honor. It was to be held at the home of a medicine man. A musician, the medicine man would also provide musical entertainment for the gala occasion. The party would begin on the afternoon of the third day after the specified guests received their invitations.

A runner was dispatched by the host to announce the invitations.

In the meantime, the host's wife prepared the all-important teshuino. An earthen pot of about five-gallons capacity was placed on a firebed of wood and nearly filled with water. Into this was tossed several handfuls of corn shoots.

The mixture was allowed to cook for the greater part of the day. It was then removed from the fire and placed in a shaded spot to ferment. The fermentation process went on for two full days. When ready for consumption, the teshuino, somewhat viscous, resembled dirty milk.

The teshuino had been set near the medicine man's lean-to for the fermentation process. The only sampling I noted was conducted by the medicine man's five-year-old son. At least four times I photographed the little urchin as he dipped grimy, brown hands into the pot and licked the milky teshuino from his fingers in wide-eyed delight.

Individuals invited to a teshuino party must earn the privilege of enjoying the host's hospitality. We were exempted from this requirement. The other guests, including Chief Pat, were put to work immediately upon their arrival.

The men cultivated the host's plot of corn, spending the day absently poking and stirring the dry clods of soil with pointed sticks. The women assisted the hostess by metating the corn into meal for the party refreshments, carrying water, and doing other household chores. One young woman sat in the shade of the lean-to hut and wove a yucca fibre basket for the hostess.

The chief stated that the type of task assigned to the male guests can vary, according to the particular host's needs and desires. They may go hunting, or fishing. There is always a need for additional firewood. Perhaps there are logs to be split into crude planks that may be needed to rebuild, or prop up, the sagging lean-to.

Shortly after noon of the third day, the teshuino was ready, the guests had completed their work, and the party was ready to begin. The men filed into the medicine man's hut and sat on their haunches, backs against the lean-to walls. The women grouped themselves about twenty yards from the hut, sitting in the shade of a tree.

A man came out of the lean-to, carrying a small gourd jar of teshuino. Walking halfway toward the circle of waiting women, who pretended to ignore his actions, he stopped and placed the jar on the ground. The Indian then quickly retreated to the sanctuary of the hut. The instant he entered the lean-to, one of the

102

women stepped forth and carried the jug of teshuino back to her group.

The formalities now completed, the party began in earnest. I sat with the men. Estelle wanted to join me, but I advised her to observe protocol and remain with the women. Jon was content to watch the party proceedings from the shade of a nearby tree.

The medicine man began the festivities by filling a small gourd bowl from the five-gallon pot of teshuino. He drank the first helping in long, slow gulps, refilled the bowl, and gave it to the chief. Using the same bowl, the host waited upon each male guest until all had been served.

When it came my turn to drink, I looked at the murky liquid, closed my eyes, and took a sip too small to swallow. I cannot adequately describe the flavor of the teshuino, except that it tasted like a thick, very green beer. I handed the bowl back to the medicine man. He placed it to his lips, tilted his head back, and drained the brew in three gulps.

After serving the initial round of teshuino, the host detailed a young man of the group to act as the waiter and bring teshuino when the thirsty Indians beckoned. I was not again offered the bowl.

The host rolled wild tobacco in a piece of dried cornhusk, lighting the bulky cylinder with a bit of wood coal. He slowly inhaled a puff and passed the cigaret to the Indian sitting to his right, who took one puff and handed it to his immediate neighbor. The cigaret was passed from man to man, like a peace pipe.

The Indian who smoked the last of the tobacco made a new cigaret, and the smoking cycle was repeated. The acrid clouds of smoke smarted my eyes and made breathing difficult. I left the lean-to and visited with the females. They were drinking teshuino and smoking wild tobacco cigarets in the same manner as their menfolk. My wife abstained.

Noting a stirring about in the lean-to, I rejoined the males. After nearly an hour of silent contemplation, and frequent lusty belts of teshuino, the sphinxlike Indians relaxed and began conversing with each other. The medicine man commenced torturing his Tarahumara violin, and the guests trooped outdoors to dance.

There was no pattern to the dance. The protesting music was without rhythm, as were the wildly gyrating Indians. They shuffled flat-footed in a single file; they frolicked mightily in tight circles; they leaped in pairs, the performers holding hands while hopping on one foot.

When the dance was finished, the Indians retired to the lean-to for a well-earned rest, and more teshuino. When the men were all inside the

104

lean-to, the women appeared and honored us with their particular dance. It was a much more subdued performance than the men's version, timidly graceful and fluid.

There is no preset time limit to a teshuino party. The Tarahumara will celebrate for as long as the teshuino and the corn cakes last. Some of these affairs will linger on for several days and nights.

Our party lasted into the night. My family and I left at dusk. Early the following morning I visited the medicine man's hut. The chief and one other straggler were still there. They and the medicine man were sitting cross-legged by the fire and looking glum. The teshuino and the corn cakes had all been consumed.

Peyote, the drug contained in the button of the mescal cactus, has been known and used by the Tarahumara for centuries. They believe that chewing the peyote bud or mixing it with teshuino will impart supernatural powers to the consumer. The canny witch doctors forbid the use of the drug by the rank and file Indians. They reserve that right for themselves, for the medicine men, and for certain invited guests.

I asked Chief Pat how he could enforce against the illegal use of peyote, especially since the Tarahumara live so widely scattered. The

105

chief said that the people's fear and superstitious respect for the witch doctor's powers make control possible. Known violators of the peyote ban are subject to instant and dire curses being imposed upon them by the witch doctor. The nature of the curses can range from corn crop failure to death from a dreaded disease. The calamitous curses are wrought by vengeful evil spirits, who are fetched from the netherworld by the witch doctor.

The Tarahumara occasionally spice the teshuino with a gruesome ingredient — pulverized human bone. A yellowed bone, crumbling from age and exposure, is brought from a burial cave. It is crushed to a fine powder on the metate, then stirred into the teshuino. There is no taboo on the use of teshuino so constituted. Any of the Tarahumara may drink it. I was unable to learn what, if any, real or fancied beneficial qualities the teshuino and bone cocktail was supposed to contain.

CHAPTER 6

Jon's plans to establish
a close rapport with the
Tarahumara teenagers
was doomed to disap-
pointment. Every one of the sixteen-year-old
boys he met had a wife, and at least one child.

The males assume the responsibilities of a husband and father as early as age thirteen. The girls become wives and mothers at eleven and twelve years of age.

There is no engagement period for a Tarahumara couple. Neither is there a wedding ceremony, as we know it. Nor do either of the partners display a token of marriage, such as a wedding ring. The parents play no part in the selection of a mate for their offspring. The girl chooses her prospective partner, and the courtship, although very hectic and unusual, is brief.

It all begins at a teshuino party. The young maiden, sitting with the other females around a campfire, looks across the way where the males are sitting around their fire, drinking teshuino, and smoking a cigaret. A young, unattached buck on whom she has had her eye for some time past has joined the group.

Searching the ground nearby, the girl gathers a supply of pebbles and small stones. She attempts to gain the unsuspecting lad's attention by pelting him with the stone ammunition. Undoubtedly the stones cause pain at impact, for they are thrown with considerable force, as well as with pinpoint accuracy.

Should the boy ignore the pebble-sniping tactics, the girl ceases throwing, at least for the time being. There will be another teshuino party,

108

and another chance at the prize. The confident maiden has plenty of time.

If the boy is interested in the girl's advances, he walks away from the campfire, ostensibly to escape the painful stone barrage. The girl leaves the circle of women and begins to stalk her prey, throwing stones at him whenever she comes within range.

Eventually, the harrassed young man breaks into a run. The Tarahumara male is probably one of the world's greatest runners, yet the pursuing female always catches him. The romance of the chase and the capture finished, the young couple seek the dubious privacy of a deserted cave or hut.

After an undisturbed honeymoon of three or four days, the newlyweds are ready to set up housekeeping, but not in a love nest they can call their own. Following long-established tribal custom, the couple will move in with the bride's parents.

The son-in-law is also required by tribal custom to obey his wife's parents, and he must dutifully respond to their every whim and command. The enforced obedience rule will remain in effect as long as either of the parents live. Failure of the groom to comply, especially with the father-in-law's demands, can result in punishment imposed by the chief.

Marriage will make little or no difference in the girl's status. After the brief honeymoon, she will resume her usual duties in the parental household. Aside from having babies, her only deviation from the normal will entail the preparation of an extra corn cake each day, to feed her mate.

Childbirth for the Tarahumara woman is a terribly primitive, often tragic, experience. Sometime during her pregnancy, the woman, or girl, selects the site where the baby will be born. She finds a tree with a lower branch growing at such a height that she must stand on tiptoe to reach it.

When it is time for delivery, the girl goes alone to the preselected tree. She makes a crude nest of leaves and grass on the ground, directly beneath the overhanging branch. Standing erect, and clutching the branch for support, she gives birth. The baby falls into the shallow nest at the mother's feet. Using two rocks in a scissorlike action, the mother severs the umbilical cord.

If, miraculously, the baby survives, and the mother does not die from hemorrhage, she will take the infant home and almost immediately carry on with her normal activities.

The Indian women use their respective "birth trees" for each successive birth. Most of the

110

babies, and many of the mothers, fail to survive the awful ordeal.

It is interesting to note the father's reaction to a blessed event. He embarks on a three day teshuino drinking celebration.

The Tarahumara are monogamous. The relationship between husband and wife is quiet and harmonious, yet strangely, there is rarely a display of affection between them. Romantic love, as eulogized in modern society, is not one of the Tarahumara's gods. In fact, *Gaw-Ree-Ma*, the only word denoting affection or love in their language, is seldom used.

A rather strict moral code is generally adhered to by the Indians. There is no wife-stealing — nor husband-luring. The rare case of adultery can be traced to a teshuino party where the chief, and his sobering influence, are not present.

It does happen that a Tarahumara husband will excuse himself from the family hearth for extended periods, sometimes for as long as two years' duration. However, he will always return to his wife and children, where his reinstatement is automatic and unquestioned.

Divorce laws, per se, do not exist in the Tarahumara society. A wife will never leave her husband. The husband can sever the marital ties on two accepted grounds: if his wife is lazy and remiss in her wifely duties, or if she talks too much.

A man cannot be punished for beating his wife, no matter how severely he may do so, provided that he was drunk at the time. If he was sober, however, he is liable to the judgment of the witch doctor.

The Tarahumara believe that a man without a wife and children cannot enter into heaven. Hence, bachelorhood is rare indeed.

Our daily association with the Tarahumara was a humbling experience. The first full week of observation convinced us that we would not find an Indian whose eyes were not dulled with the opaqueness of constant hunger.

Wherever we ranged throughout the land we found the Indians living in terrible squalor — diseased, hungry, hopeless, but uncomplaining. It was heartbreaking for us to see the potbellied, famished children. The disease-scabbed lips of these unfortunate little creatures would never peal the music of childish laughter — that delightful sound inspired by robust, young health and the pure joy of just being alive.

Determined to help the destitute Indians, we met with Chief Pat for a late evening conference. We wanted his help in transporting supplies of food from the general store at Panaluchic Mis-

112

sion, and distributing them to the families in the vicinity of our camp. The chief said that he would arrange for someone to go after the supplies.

I gave him a slip of paper which listed in Spanish an order for 200 pounds of corn, 100 pounds of beans, 50 pounds of salt, and 25 one-pound bars of strong soap. I also gave him a sheaf of pesos to cover the cost of the provisions.

The chief summoned his son-in-law from within the hut. He spoke briefly with him and handed him the note and the money. The boy left at a fast trot, disappearing into the early darkness. I supposed that he had gone to find several Indians to help him, and that they would leave in the morning for the mission store. It was indeed a surprise to learn from the chief that the lad was on his way to Panaluchic, and that he would bring back the supplies without help.

Twenty-four hours later, as dusk was melting swiftly into darkness, the young Indian returned, leading three packsaddled burros laden with the articles we had ordered. Bringing the weary burros to a halt, the boy handed me the original order list and the change left from the transaction. He had procured everything on the list, and the change was exact to the last centavo.

Jon and I helped unload the pack saddles and carry the supplies into the schoolroom. The

113

Indian led the burros to the river's edge. He turned the tired and hungry animals loose to drink and graze on the scattered clumps of bunchgrass. The boy then ran to his home.

An hour later, he returned and rounded up the three burros. We asked him where he was taking the animals, and he said that he was returning them to the owners in Panaluchic. My questions as to how he had managed to borrow the pack animals were answered with a noncommittal shrug of the shoulders.

The following morning, I went to Chief Pat's lean-to. Standing nonchalantly in front of the hut was his son-in-law. I was amazed. Since eight o'clock the prior evening, the young Indian had led the burros to Panaluchic and had run back to his hut in time to catch forty winks before sunrise.

The remarkable feat had been accomplished over a very rugged route, involving a round trip of nearly sixty miles. And this was done during the hours of a moonless night. It was another unbelievable demonstration of the Tarahumara's tremendous running capabilities.

I asked Chief Pat to accept the supplies and to dole them out equally among the Indians. The chief refused, saying that *we* should give away the corn, beans, salt, and soap. He said

114

that he would stand by and supervise the full operation.

The chief's son-in-law was dispatched to summon the people from the surrounding area. Within three hours after the messenger had departed, the first Indians began to arrive. Throughout that first day, all through the night, and the following morning, they trickled in from every point of the compass. There were but few children among them.

The Indians did not congregate. They selected widely separated places to settle and await further developments. There was no festive note in their behavior. They did not visit with each other, nor did they come by to greet or stare at us.

By noon of the second day, thirty-five Tarahumara men and women were clustered around the schoolhouse grounds. The chief said that except for several stragglers, there would be no more. We were ready to dispense the supplies. Using a cup to measure and pour the corn, beans, and salt, and a knife to slice the bars of soap, Estelle and Jon gave the Indians equal shares as they shuffled by in single file.

The people had a unique and puzzling method of carrying the supplies. Each removed a twisted piece of dirty cloth from about his waist and spread it upon the ground in front of Estelle

115

and Jon. On this the share of food, salt, and soap was placed in separate piles. The cloth was then deftly and quickly folded into a small packet. Later, when the packet was unfolded, the contents would be unmixed, just as though they had been placed in individual, sealed containers.

The Indians accepted their individual shares without a word. As they silently filed past, the softened and warm look in their normally expressionless eyes was the only token of appreciation we received — or needed.

Watching them depart for their far-flung homes, it seemed to me that their steps were a little higher, their backs a bit straighter, and their arms swinging with more freedom than when they had come to us.

There was one disquieting incident which occurred during the distribution of the supplies. Chief Pat, Eppie, and I were standing aside, watching the proceedings. The chief stepped away from me and ran to a young man to whom Jon had just given a portion of corn and beans. His face in an ugly scowl, Chief Pat swiftly snatched the bounty from the frightened Indian's hands and gave it back to Jon.

With Eppie at my side, I joined the chief and asked what had happened and why he had taken the food away from the Indian boy. Still vividly angry, the chief pointed to the lad and

116

said, in effect, "He is strong. He will not plant corn, nor will he hunt and fish. He does not eat!"

No amount of persuasion on our part could alter the chief's decision. In fact, he turned his wrath on me when I persisted in arguing for the offending Indian.

Harsh and shocking as the incident was to my family and me, it at least revealed an important facet of Tarahumara philosophy. The Indians will care for the widowed, the orphaned, and the elderly to the best of their limited abilities; but they will permit no compromise with the bitter realities. The able-bodied males must shift for themselves — or perish.

Chief Pat was full of surprises. The day after we had given the supplies away, he came to us and announced that the Tarahumara were going to stage a feast in our honor. We were completely flabbergasted. A feast? I asked the chief what the people were going to use for food.

He informed us that food was really no problem. The Indians would prepare the corn and beans we had given! We argued that it would be the better part of wisdom if the people would forget about honoring us with a dinner, and concentrate instead on saving the precious corn and beans for darker days ahead.

117

Chief Pat's muleheaded stubborness leaped to the fore. He stated most emphatically that, even without our approval, the feast would be held.

We did not want to offend the childlike Indians. We also realized that these poor people rarely had occasion to celebrate anything during their miserable lives. Our protests ceased, and we informed the chief that we would be very happy to attend the planned festivities. Chief Pat was pleased. His dour face softened, and we were rewarded with one of his rare smiles.

The feast was scheduled to begin on a Sunday morning at the site of the old mission ruins. Afterwards, there would be native dancing, and also a running of the *rarahipa*, or kickball race. The race was to be especially staged for our entertainment. We were overjoyed, for we had literally given up hope of watching and photographing one of these much talked about events.

Estelle, Jon, and I stood to one side and discussed the forthcoming feast. We came to the unanimous conclusion that corn and beans alone would not suffice for a banquet, not even a primitive one. Meat should be served as the pièce de résistance. But where would we get the meat?

The chief vetoed a hunt. He said that the the possibility of bagging a deer, or other game, was uncertain on such short notice. We suggest-

118

ed a goat. Yes, the people would be delighted to feast on goat meat. The chief said he knew where one might be obtained, but it would require many pesos.

I thust a wad of bills into his hand and urged him to procure the goat. As we had learned to expect, the task was delegated to his son-in-law, who left at once, running up the deep canyon that led toward Panaluchic.

At dawn the next morning the young man and the chief, pulling and pushing a large, lean, and very disturbed goat, presented themselves at our camp. The chief tied the goat to a tree and gave me change from the transaction. The animal had cost the sum of 50 pesos ($4).

The men began to assemble at the feast grounds Saturday afternoon. Those Indians whom we had not seen before gave our camp a wide berth on their way to the mission ruins area, located about a hundred yards from us.

Significantly, the men whom we had previously met, either at their homes or during the recent teshuino party, passed quite near on their way to join the other arrivals. They walked by slowly, courting our attention and acknowledging our greetings with a shy smile, or a softly murmured *"Quee-Ra-Ba!"*

We were highly elated. After many discouraging efforts to thaw the withdrawn and hostile

119

Tarahumara, we at last were "getting through" to them, and being accepted.

Only a few of the women came to the mission grounds during the day. They isolated themselves in a distant group, associating neither with the Indian men, nor with us. The remainder of the females would not arrive until after nightfall. They would spend the day, and a part of the night, in their huts, busily metating and preparing the corn dishes they would bring to the feast. (With the inclusion of the goat meat on the menu, the beans were eliminated.)

Few in number, particularly in the more remote areas, goats are held in high regard by the Tarahumara. The meat of the animal is not a regular part of the Indian's diet. It is reserved for religious ceremonies and other significant tribal affairs.

Goat hides are important, providing untanned leather for sandals, lacings, papoose cradles, and covers for the ceremonial drums. The skins also serve as prime items of bartering value at the various mission stores.

The slaughter of the goat we donated toward the feast seemed to have sacrificial import, and it easily held the forefront in the day's proceedings.

In midafternoon, the chief summoned the men to gather at the tree where the goat was tied.

At the chief's command, two men stepped from the group and untied the animal. Holding the front and rear legs, they stretched the mute beast full length upon the ground.

A large, flat rock was fetched from the hillside and placed beneath the goat's shoulder. Two more Indians, one holding a large gourd bowl, posted themselves at the prone animal's head. When these preliminaries had been completed, the chief requested Jon's sharp hunting knife, which was then relayed to one of the men squatting by the goat's neck.

Swiftly, expertly, the Indian pierced the goat's jugular, capturing the crimson flow in the gourd bowl. When the last of the blood had dripped into the container, the men holding the goat's legs released their grip. They returned to the group of Indians who had been silently and intently watching the slaughter ritual.

Each person who participated in the killing, dressing, and cooking of the goat was to be rewarded. The man who had dispatched the goat left the scene, proudly and carefully carrying the rim-filled bowl of blood. I did not learn of the ultimate disposition of the blood. Presumably, the Indian and his family drank it.

One man was designated by the chief to skin and dress the animal and carve the carcass into

121

small pieces. When his task was completed, the chief presented the man with the entrails.

The two Indians who had imprisoned the goat to the ground were rewarded with the lungs and tongue. The skin was given to a young man. He was appointed to build and maintain the wood fire over which the goat meat was to be cooked.

A lone woman shared in the prizes. After her nightlong and smoke-filled chore of tending the cooking pot, she received the bones, from which every shred of meat had been removed for the feast. Some time after the feast, when the hunger pains returned, the woman would crush the bones and meticulously pick them clean of nutritious marrow. The extraction completed, the splintered remains would become the property of the family dog.

Because he was the chief, Pat reserved the goat's heart and liver for himself.

Starlight had replaced dusk when the chunks of goat meat were placed in a large clay pot containing water. The pot was propped on four rocks, directly over the curling flames of a wood fire. The woman assigned to tend the meat began her all-night vigil.

The young man detailed as the fire-keeper fed fresh fuel to the fire as needed, procuring the wood from a heap he had gathered before dark.

122

With the exception of the chief, all of the men who would be on hand for the feast were on the grounds by midnight. The women continued to arrive, singly and in pairs, throughout the night.

Among the more than fifty Tarahumara who came to the feast, only six were children. Two were babies, the rest were less than six years of age.

Unperturbed by the activities, and assured that his interpretive services would not be needed, Eppie went to sleep shortly after dark.

My family and I retired at midnight. Jon slept soundly. Estelle napped fitfully. I was very tired, but a strange restlessness besieged me, and I could not sleep. Frequently during the long night I arose and went outside to stand in the eerie solitude and ponder on the lonely, primitive scene.

The stars blinked coldly from a blue-black vault of sky. A chill breeze teased the small campfires burning on the shelfland and on the banks of the river below. The flickering light of the fires silhouetted forlorn Indians sleeping on the ground or sitting hunched by the campfires.

As the first light of dawn etched the outline of the peaks and crags across the Río Conchos, I shouldered my camera, stuffed some flashbulbs into my pocket, and went to where the goat was being cooked. I wanted to observe and photo-

123

graph the woman cook as she completed the final stages of her assigned task.

She and the fire-keeper had removed the blackened pot from the fire. I watched as she reached both hands into the container and fished the meat from the still hot broth. There was enough overcooked meat to fill four large gourd bowls.

The bones had already been retrieved from the pot. Picked clean of meat, they were piled on the ground. When the woman sieved the last shred of meat from the broth with her fingers, she lay down beside the meat-filled bowls and went to sleep. It had been a long night.

Seeing the preparation of the goat meat made me determined to circumvent the honor of sharing in the Indians' banquet. I returned to Estelle and Jon, awakened them, and we ate a hurried breakfast.

I yelled at Eppie to wake up and join us, and we went to the area fronting the former mission. We found Pat and the rest of the Indians standing quietly in small groups, as though they were awaiting our arrival.

Chief Pat made a motion with his arms toward the waiting Indians. The women and children went to one end of the clearing and sat on the ground in a tight circle. In the center a small fire burned. About seventy feet from the women, the men squatted in a large circle around their fire.

124

Chief Pat stationed himself midway between the two groups. On the ground beside him were the four bowls heaped with goat meat, the clay cookpot containing the goat broth, a huge pile of precooked corn cakes, and a type of corn food which resembled a fat tamale.

Prepared only for special occasions, the corn tamales were made of a heavy, unsalted dough kneaded from cracked corn and water. Rolled into cylindrical shapes about six inches long and two inches in diameter, each was wrapped in green corn leaves. The rolls had been boiled in their leafy blankets the preceding night. Except for peeling off the soggy leaves, they were ready to eat. There were enough corn rolls on hand to allow one serving per person.

The Indians did not come forward to help themselves to the food. They waited for the chief to serve them. We were surprised to see the chief wait upon the women first. It was strange, indeed, to behold the haughty Pat submit to the role of a servant to his people. With a humility that failed to tarnish his stature and dignity as the chief, he hurried from one individual to another, giving each an equal share of food.

My family and I politely refused our portions of the banquet. I explained that photographing the people during the feasting would keep my family and me too busy to eat. The

125

chief accepted my excuse gracefully, and without argument.

The Indians did not begin eating until Chief Pat had served everyone and had given the signal for them to commence. They fell to with concentrated gusto, interrupted only by the sudden flashes of bright light, as I took numerous pictures of the happy yet solemn scene.

The rising sun was caressing the land when the Indians had finished eating. Even greater than the sun's revealing illumination was the light that glowed on the faces of the assembled Tarahumara. Their stomachs pleasantly full, they would now enjoy a few short hours of contentment and well-being before the return of the familiar, nagging pains of hunger.

After the feast we returned to our small room in the church annex. For the first time, we had a constant stream of visitors. No longer afraid, the Indians were content to stand or sit quietly nearby and watch our personal activities.

Estelle unwittingly provided the curious onlookers with humorous entertainment when she stepped outside to brush her teeth. The combination of facial contortions, vigorous brushing, paste foam, spitting, and lusty gargling, caused the enraptured audience to point their fingers at my embarrassed wife and howl with glee.

My subsequent public shaving act held poor

126

second billing to Estelle's performance. Instead of laughter, it provoked some serious discussions among the Indians, plus dubious head shakes, and some rather strange looks cast my way.

Among our visitors was a pretty, thirteen-year-old bride and her good-looking, fourteen-year-old husband. The children had been married only a few weeks. Following the pattern of the other Indians who came by to see us, the shy couple chose a vantage point a short distance from our open doorway, where they sat apart and intently watched our every move.

I tried to persuade either, or both, of the bashful youngsters to come to our door. My clumsy efforts were in vain. Estelle's approach was uncomplicated, and direct: she simply went to the girl, took her by the hand, and led her into our room.

Estelle searched her pack and produced a pair of simple, bright red earrings. She gently fastened the baubles to the girl's ears and held up a small mirror — the first the Indian girl had ever seen. The simple ingredients of two red earrings, plus one mirror, provided an easy recipe for instant and overwhelming happiness. Smiling radiantly, the excited girl-wife turned from the looking glass and ran swiftly to show the wondrous pendants to her husband.

127

In appreciation for Estelle's gift to his wife, the grateful husband offered me his bright yellow cloth headband. I, in turn, gave him a large red bandanna, which he immediately folded into a narrow band, and tied around his head.

Throughout the day, the Indian girl came often to our doorway to stand and smile at Estelle. She would alternately point to the pack which she knew contained the mirror, and then reach to touch the precious red bubbles of glass clasped to her ears. In the only way that she knew, the girl was telling Estelle that she wanted yet another view of herself in the magic glass.

CHAPTER 7

A group of Indians, accompanied by Chief Pat, came to me. Pat explained that he had been talking to the men about my crossbow, and they wanted a demonstration of its accuracy and power.

129

I selected a tree with a backdrop free of wandering Indians. Standing about thirty yards away, I shot four arrows in rapid succession. My luck held, and I placed them all in a neat cluster in the center of the tree trunk.

The Indians watched every detail of my performance with intense interest. When the last arrow thudded into the tree bark, they looked at me with wide-eyed approval and converged on the target. The steel points of the arrows were imbedded, out of sight, in the wood. I whittled the heads free with my bowie knife, and gave the arrows to the Indians as souvenirs.

All of the Indians wanted to shoot the cross-bow, but only the chief was allowed to try his luck at the target. His score was two arrows widely spaced on the trunk of the tree. The third one had missed the target completely. It was deeply buried in the ground beyond the tree.

The chief was delighted with the results. I was very proud of him. Totally unfamiliar with the sighting and shooting of the strange weapon, he had hit the target with two out of three arrows. The lone miss did nothing to injure his native pride.

After the target shooting, I fired two arrows for maximum distance, sending them winging over the top of a high ridge more than three hundred yards away. It is almost impossible for

130

the eye to follow a crossbow arrow in flight, and I had no idea where the arrows would eventually land.

I indicated that the demonstration was finished. Two Indians ran toward the ridge and disappeared in the tangled brush and jumbled rocks at the base of the hill. An hour and a half later, they came running back. Breathing easily, they handed me the battered remains of the two arrows. The chief questioned them briefly and then told me that the Indians had located the arrows in the rocks on the opposite side of the ridge.

How they had managed to find the arrows was a mystery. It was an amazing performance, and one that was to be repeated several times at other demonstrations by Tarahumara chosen at random from eager volunteers. For their efforts, I gave the happy retrievers the broken and useless arrows.

Youths the world over dream of the day when they will become men. Recognition of this achievement varies among the different cultures. Among certain tribes of New Guinea, for example, a stripling becomes a man when he can venture forth alone and return to his village bearing a neighboring tribesman's head on a spear. In many lands, a youngster assumes the responsibilities of manhood as soon as he can till the soil. American lads are considered to be full-fledged men when they are old enough to cast a ballot.

To qualify as a man, a Tarahumara boy undergoes an extreme physical endurance test. He must complete, nonstop, a cross-country run of at least one hundred miles, between the hours of sunrise and sunset.

Having passed this rugged test, the new man is eligible to compete in the all-important rarahipa, or kickball race. It is of interest to note that nearly all fifteen-year-old Tarahumara males are qualified to run in the rarahipa.

Two groups of men compete in the rarahipa, the Tarahumara's only competitive team sport. The total number of men participating will vary according to the length and importance of the contest. However, each team must field an equal number of runners.

The teams each have a kickball, carved from juniper wood, and slightly larger than a baseball. Racing cross-country toward a goal that is seldom less than twenty-five miles from the starting point, the barefoot teams strive to be the first to kick their semihardwood ball over the finish line.

All rarahipas are run nonstop. There are no relays or reliefs. In a major event, as many as one hundred men will run a race of one hundred and seventy-five miles or more. Beginning at mid-

132

morning of a given day, the ordeal will be completed by early afternoon of the next day.

The Tarahumara's incredible running feats in the terrible conglomerate of the barranca country border on the unbelievable. When darkness overtakes the fleet runners, noncompeting Indians carry pine torches and run with the teams. The flickering yellow lights of the torches help the kickers to follow the balls, and also assist them in locating the kickballs when they become wedged in a maze of rocks, lost in heavy brush, or imbedded in a patch of spiny cactus.

During the course of a rarahipa, the players receive nourishment and water from runners stationed at strategic intervals along the way.

The in-play rules of the sport are few and are obeyed by the players without the supervision of a referee. The contestants must propel the ball with their bare feet the entire distance of the race. If the ball becomes so lodged in a natural obstruction that it cannot be kicked free, it may be picked up with the hand and dropped in a playable position.

The running of the rarahipa, even in the short versions, exacts a painful, often serious, toll from many of the participants. Nails are frequently torn completely away from cruelly battered toes. Broken feet, which are left untreated, heal in twisted deformities, sometimes leaving the victim crippled for life. Deeply lacerated flesh wounds of the feet and legs become infected and often gangrenous. When this happens, death is inevitable.

The rarahipa is never staged purely for sport alone. Prior to the start of a race, the contestants and their many backers contribute to a "jackpot" prize of corn, beans, cloth, skins, anything considered of value. The stakes are vied for on a "winner-take-all" basis. The spoils are divided equally among the members of the winning team.

The Indians who do not run in the rarahipa avidly place personal side bets on the outcome of the race. Needless to say, the penchant for wagering their meagre foodstocks can frequently have punishing effects upon the losers.

Shortly after noon of the feast day, the Tarahumara began organizing for the rarahipa. Although this was to be a short-distance race, staged for our enlightenment and entertainment, it nevertheless generated a great excitement among the gathered Indians. Every man present wanted to run.

As usual, Chief Pat took charge. He selected two men from the anxious group, explaining to me that they were the best rarahipa runners in the district. The men were designated by the chief to select their respective team members,

134

whom they would lead in the forthcoming contest. Each team was to consist of three runners, including the leader.

The formalities of team selection and organization were quickly completed, and the Indians focused their attention on making up a prize purse for the rarahipa winners.

Most of the available corn had been contributed toward the morning feast. However, the beans and salt we had given to the Indians were still on hand. A major portion of this would have gone into the rarahipa jackpot, but we argued with Chief Pat to let us donate the prizes for the winning racers.

We won that round, but ultimately lost the fight. Relieved of the burden of providing for a jackpot, the happy primitives were now in a more favorable position to make personal wagers on their favorite team. We resigned ourselves to the inevitable and made no further efforts to interfere.

Whether by design or coincidence, the chief's son-in-law was selected as one of the team runners. Chief Pat placed his bet of beans and salt on his son-in-law's team.

The team leaders, or captains, each had a small hollowed gourd, the narrow neck stoppered with a plug of corncob. The smooth, yellowed gourds each contained several round pebbles about the size of marbles. Suspended from a rawhide thong tied around the wearer's lean waist, the gourd rested on the captain's backside. The gourd bounced and rolled with each step or sudden movement of the team leader and caused the pebbles inside to tumble. The resultant sharp, castanetlike clatter was clearly audible a hundred yards away.

Chief Pat explained that the gourds were normally worn only during the long races that extended throughout the night. As the rarahipa progresses, the runners have a tendency to become widely separated. The team leader is generally up front, and the staccato clatter of the gourds serves as a constant sound beacon for those stragglers running far behind. The gourds also serve to warn anyone loitering in the path of the rarahipa to get out of the way.

The race was to start at the open area fronting the mission ruins. It was three o'clock in the afternoon when the team captains kicked off, sending the juniper kickballs flying and bouncing one hundred and fifty feet along the course. Before the balls stopped rolling, runners dashed up and kicked them forward on the next stage of the race. The Indians do not kick the ball directly with their toes, but propel it with the instep. Curiously, they are able to do this without sacrificing speed or breaking the rhythm of their

136

forward pace. The severe foot and toe injuries sustained by the rarahipa runners are undoubtedly caused by the accidental kicking and stubbing of rocks, rather than from direct toe contact with the ball.

I have always prided myself on my speed and endurance afoot, and I intended to run with the Indians and photograph the highlights of the action. The runners disappeared from sight before I completed the first two hundred yards. I returned to Chief Pat's side and tried to hide my embarrassment.

Leaving the mission area, the Tarahumara proceeded up the steep canyon that led to Panaluchic. At a predesignated point, the runners turned about and kicked the balls back toward Tehuerichic, crossing the Río Conchos in front of and below our vantage point.

Kicking the balls across the river barrier, the racers continued onward, streaming over a steep mountain and beyond to the entrance of a small barranca. Again reversing their field, the Indians came back across the river and on up the hill to the old mission grounds, where the fifteen mile contest came to an end.

The first team crossed the finish line two and one-half hours after the start of the rarahipa. The losers came in ten minutes later, very dejected indeed.

The runners, sweating and dust covered, showed no signs of fatigue. They stood about, relaxed and completely at ease, breathing quietly, without so much as a yawn. The only discomfiture was exhibited by the losers. Ignored by their fellows, they stood apart, downcast and ashamed. Perhaps the chief's son-in-law was the most chagrined of all. He was one of the losers.

We rewarded the proud winners with items of food and red bandannas. Breaking Tarahumara custom, we also gave food to the losers. Chief Pat made no verbal protests, but he was obviously displeased at our behavior. When he left much later that evening, he was still miffed at us.

As the chief walked toward the river on his way home, we saw that his son-in-law was also being treated to a sample of Pat's displeasure. Instead of walking beside his father-in-law, as was his custom, the young man was following at least fifty feet behind.

By far the outstanding feature of the Tarahumara Indians is their ability to run tremendous distances in a land so formidable that an "outsider" finds walking extremely difficult and exhausting.

Considering the primitive life, the abject poverty, the disease and malnutrition that exacts such a fearful toll from them all, how can the

138

average Tarahumara boy of fifteen run one hundred miles nonstop, in one day? Seeking the answer, a number of American medical specialists visited Mission Sisoguichic during the summer of 1968. Headed by Dr. Reed S. Clegg, of Salt Lake City, Utah, the team of doctors made extensive tests and physical examinations of the Tarahumara.

The studies produced some interesting conclusions, which will be published in book form. The results of these studies are also being made available to the United States Olympic Committee.

The medical findings, in a summary for the layman, are herein quoted from a letter received by the author from Doctor Clegg:

> We feel that the ability of the Indians to run the way they can, is due to heredity, and environment. They have had to participate in this way, in order to live.
>
> They practice this sport from early childhood, and keep at it routinely. They have developed measures of smooth automation, and when repeated day after day, this becomes a routine way of life.
>
> Their congenitally low blood pressure, and pulse rate, permit them to participate much better. They also have kept their weight down, which is essential.
>
> As far as nutrition is concerned, beans, corn, and a moderate amount of meat suffice. The main thing is that they do not gourmetize.

139

Extremely popular among the Tarahumara is a game curiously akin to our horseshoe-pitching contests.

A circular hole, about five inches in diameter and two inches in depth, is chipped into an outcropping of flat rock with a flint chisel. In the same or a similar outcropping thirty to fifty feet away, a like hole is formed. The two holes, or cups, are the game goals.

The opposing players take their positions at each hole. The object of the game is to toss a semiround stone with a flat base into the opposite cup. The player whose stone lands in the cup is the game winner.

Since the stones are only slightly smaller in circumference than the cups in the rock bases, a great deal of skill and considerable strength is required to throw them so that they will land, bounce, or slide into the cups. (A comparison would be a golfer sinking a fifty-foot chip shot.)

One afternoon, Chief Pat came to our camp and awakened me from a restful nap. He asked if my family and I would like to accompany him downriver a couple of miles, where the medicine man and another Indian would shortly conduct a rain dance. We responded with alacrity. Under a blue and cloudless sky, we almost ran the entire distance, afraid that we might miss the performance.

We found the rain dancers making final preparations for the ritual. The medicine man was putting the finishing touches to a crude wooden cross he had fashioned from two sticks of wood that measured no more than four inches in length. I was unable to learn the role that the small cross would play in the intricacies of the rain dance.

Near the medicine man stood a large gourd partially filled with teshuino. Finished with the wooden cross, he tucked it into his loincloth and picked up the teshuino jar. His assistant cocked the bow over the strings of the violin he held jammed into his waist.

With the first protesting screech from the violin, the men began to dance in a tight circle. Their heads were thrown back, and they cried loud incantations to the stingy rain god.

The circling phase of the dance lasted about five minutes. The musician played the violin throughout, and the medicine man frequently reached a hand into the jar and threw offerings of teshuino into the air.

Hopping and shuffling, the dancers moved down a small arroyo, coming to a halt in an area that was free of rocks and boulders. Still chanting and pleading to the rain god, the medicine man sprayed more of the teshuino into the air above him. His partner placed the violin on

141

the ground, removed his headband and shirt, and flung them violently away from him. He resumed playing the violin, his eyes staring fixedly at the blue vault of sky.

When the jug was finally emptied of teshuino, it was placed on the ground. The medicine man withdrew the wooden cross from his loincloth and hurled it high into the air. The cross was immediately followed by his headband and shirt.

The two men gyrated wildly for a few moments, uttered a torrent of high-pitched, garbled words, and fell limply to the ground. The rain dance was over. The final result was now up to the revered rain god.

During the rain dance, I especially watched the faces of the two Indians. They appeared to be in a trance when we arrived at the dance site, and they gave no hint, then or thereafter, that they were aware of us or their immediate surroundings. It was as though they were drugged with peyote, or under the influence of teshuino. It was my studied impression that they were under the effects of both. As the ritual progressed toward its finale, their hypnosis, or spell, deepened. When it was all over, the confrontation with the rain god left them spent, their faces agonized and contorted. They walked about like confused robots.

142

We returned to camp, sobered by the raw display of primitive emotions. At dawn on the following morning, we were deluged with a downpour of rain. The mighty rain god had spoken.

CHAPTER 8

Although Death, the insatiable grim reaper, works overtime among them, the Tarahumara await their individual rendezvous with him calmly, almost with eagerness. Chief Pat summarized

145

the Indian's outlook on death concisely. He said, "We won't hunger anymore."

There is no family or tribal mourning at the death of a Tarahumara. The Indians do not conduct funeral services, hold death rites, or make special preparations of the deceased's body for burial.

The clothing is removed from the body; it will be used again by the living. Adult male members or relatives of the immediate family carry the corpse to the burial cave. The simple task of depositing the body in the burial cave completed, the Indians will return to their homes, and life will go on as though the deceased had never existed.

After the death of a Tarahumara head of a household, his widow and children (if there are any), become the responsibility of the departed's son-in-law. In the event there is no son-in-law, an adult son, brother, or even a grandfather must assume the responsibility.

I wondered if there would be any ban on our visiting a burial cave. The chief said that there are no tribal or sacred taboos connected with Tarahumara burial caves. He added that if we so desired, he would be happy to escort us to the nearest site, about three miles from our camp.

The burial cave was located about one thousand feet above the Río Conchos, on the steep north side of the river canyon. It was a difficult climb. As we panted slowly upward toward the mouth of the cave, I could visualize several Indians struggling up the incline, bearing the body of one of their dead to its eternal rest.

With the abundance of more readily available caves on both sides of the rock-walled river, I wondered why the Tarahumara had chosen the particular one above us.

As Pat led us nearer to the burial cave, we saw human skeletal parts scattered haphazardly about the hillside: a bleached and fractured leg-bone wedged between two rocks, a rib cage resting against the gnarled trunk of a stunted scrub oak, a cracked and yellowed skull leering at us from beneath a low cactus bush. Disquieting as the gruesome approach had been, we were to be appalled at the grisly scene that awaited us inside the unsealed tomb.

We entered the cave, with the chief leading the way. Inside, it was damp and semidark. The pale light revealed a large, deep cave, with a low, domed ceiling. The lower portion of the dark-brown rock walls was a ghostly grey. The floor was a conglomerate of skulls, bones, gravel, and numerous large, flat stones.

The gravel and the stones were brought into the cave when it was first put to use for burials, countless years before. As the years and the burials

147

went by, additional gravel and stones were brought in as needed. The original cave floor was now about five feet below the accumulation of rocky material and bones.

When a body is brought to the cave, a small trough is scooped with the hands in the surface of the gravel. The cadaver is laid in the trough and barely covered with the gravel. The heavy, flat stones are placed on the corpse as a deterrent to the wild animals that enter the cave and feed on the dead. The bones scattered about the hillside below the cave mouth, and the gnawed and splintered ones inside, indicated the futility of the stone anchors.

Chief Pat said that other caves in his area were regularly used by his people as burial places. He said that the cave we were visiting was not often used, the most recent burials there being that of a young girl whom the evil spirits had killed with disease, and that of an adult male who had died of starvation the preceding winter.

Jon was intrigued by the burial cave. While he was examining a particular bone, he discovered a curious ornament lying in the gravel. Made of a rock that looked like soapstone, it had been chipped by flint into a circular shape, about one inch in diameter; a hole had been cut in the middle of the stone. Chief Pat said that at one time the Tarahumara strung a series of such stones on rawhide or cactus fibre and wore them about the neck. At death, this necklace was the only item that was buried with the owner.

While inspecting the various skulls in the cave, Jon found one that especially interested him. It was in good condition, and he asked me if he might keep it and bring it home. Not wanting to make a mistake that could cause us to become permanent guests in that awful cave, I referred Jon's request to the chief.

Chief Pat readily granted Jon's request. In fact, we could take with us as many bones as we liked. The chief added a word of warning: if the bones were not happy wherever we took them, they would return to the burial cave.

Estelle was understandably nervous while in the cave. However, she squeamishly held a long bone gingerly between her thumb and forefinger, and posed with Jon and his newly acquired skull, for a burial cave picture.

The Tarahumara believe in a reincarnation. Much of what Chief Pat told me about this was lost in translation. However, I was able to gather that the Indian's second life would be in the form of a bird. I was unable to learn into just what species of bird this rebirth would be.

Interestingly, the macaw, a member of the parrot family, is one of the Tarahumara gods, the god of judgment. If an Indian sees a macaw

149

sitting on a tree limb and the raucous bird yells at him, the superstitious primitive believes that judgment has been pronounced upon him. His days are numbered, and the Indian is convinced that death is imminent, and unescapable.

En route back to camp from the burial cave, Chief Pat took us on one of his inevitable detours. This time he led us to the site of his winter home. The cave was in the base of a cliff, facing the Río Conchos.

The chief posed proudly for a photograph in front of the cave, which was the largest and most pretentious of all the caves we had seen. It was certainly the most unusual, for it had another, equally large cave directly above the ground level one. Chief Pat was the owner of probably the only two-story cave dwelling in the Tarahumara barranca country.

The chief escorted us through the interior of the lower cave. High and wide, it was roomy enough to have accommodated at least six families. The cave was damp, and had a dank odor. Pat said that during the rainy season most of the area caves, including his, leaked badly, with the water seeping through and dripping from the fire-blackened, fissured rock ceiling.

Except for the ever-present stone metate in one corner, the cave was empty. The chief explained

150

that the Tarahumara do not take the metates with them when they make their seasonal moves from cave to hut, and back (when winter approaches). The stones are large, and, of course, too heavy to transport back and forth. It is much simpler to make a metate for each place of residence.

The second-story cave was about twenty feet above the lower one. Access was by way of a natural, sloping ledge on the cliff face. The upper opening was much smaller than the bottom cave entrance, but the interiors were of equal size.

I asked Chief Pat if he utilized the upper cave. He said that it was used for the storage of corn and personal possesions during the winter months.

On the back wall of the cave I saw a curious object. Made of river mud and small stones, it was shaped like a large cone. Its three-foot-diameter base was mud-mortared to the rough rock wall, and was about four feet above the floor.

The strange-looking cone was built horizontal to the cave floor. At its apex was a round opening approximately a foot in diameter. The entire contraption resembled a very large mud dauber's nest. Pat explained that the cone was built as a toad-proof storage place for the family's winter supply of corn.

In the course of our travels about the barrancas and along the banks of the Río Conchos, I had picked up some bits of gold-bearing ore. I asked Chief Pat if he knew what gold was. He did, but added that the Tarahumara were not infected with the white man's gold fever, that the yellow metal was a prime instrument of serious trouble.

I asked the chief if any white men ever came into the barranca country seeking gold. He related that several years previously a man had come into the Tehuerichic region alone and had looked for gold. The intruder did not realize it, but the Indians kept constant vigil on the prospector.

One day, the prospector found gold. After a week of digging, he decided he had all that he could successfully carry, and he started the long trek back to the "outside." Before he departed the site of his find, the man carefully marked the area for future reference.

Proceeding up a narrow, boulder-strewn canyon, the man was seized by four Tarahumara. Using the prospector's hunting knife, they cut off his hands and left him to die. The Indians took the gold and threw it into the Río Conchos. They also destroyed the markers of the place where the gold had been found.

I was shocked by the account, even more so by the chief's grim countenance and manner as he told it. I asked if cutting off the prospector's hands wasn't perhaps too drastic. The chief did not think so. As he put it, "He won't dig any more gold!"

The rain that had fallen every morning since the Tarahumara's recent and fervent supplications to the rain god became increasingly heavier, and longer in duration. It would be foolhardy for us to remain any longer than necessary. It was obvious that the annual rainy season was getting an early start.

A prolonged deluge, flooding the labyrinth of deep canyons that lay between us and Sisoguichic, would assuredly strand us indefinitely. I told Chief Pat that we would leave at dawn, three days hence. He did not reply, but I could see the sudden sadness in his face.

The day before our scheduled departure, we were paid a surprise visit by the Tarahumara who lived in the surrounding area. Chief Pat had passed the word, and the same crowd that had attended the feast, plus a few strangers, gathered to wish us a farewell.

The men and women stood in the traditional separate groups and faced us in silence as Chief Pat told my family and me that, because we had befriended his people, and had given them food, all of the Tarahumara would always be our

153

friends, and that they would await the day of our welcome return.

The primitive chieftain then paid me the highest compliment I could have received. He said, "You are like Father Laguna."

I was making preparations to photograph Chief Pat as he stood in front of the assembled men. Estelle asked me to wait. Impulsively, she ran to the cluster of watching women. Taking the chief's wife and the little girl-wife with the red earrings by the hand, she led them to the all-male gathering, and posed with the females by the side of the surprised chief.

Chief Pat said nothing. He remained impassive. The reaction among the other Indian men was mixed. Some grumbled openly at the intrusion. The others remained silent, but the dark scowls revealed their acute displeasure.

After I had taken several pictures, the gathering disbanded, and the Indians went their separate ways homeward, the individual helpmeets following them at a discreet distance.

The chief was not his usual self. He left brusquely, saying that he would see me in the morning. Estelle wondered if he were angry with her for breaking the strict Tarahumara protocol regarding the separation of the sexes.

I was of the opinion that Chief Pat was contemplating our departure the next dawn.

154

Genuinely fond of us, he did not want us to leave.

The chief's wife and the girl with the red earrings came to Estelle to say good-bye, for we would not see them again before we left. The girl reached for Estelle's extended hand, held it briefly, and bashfully departed, occasionally stopping to look back.

Chief Pat's wife presented Estelle with ten small, beautifully woven reed baskets that she had made the day before. She pressed Estelle's hand in farewell, and with downcast eyes walked slowly away.

At dawn the following morning, we had stowed our packs, filled our canteens with water, and were ready for the trail. There was a slight rain falling, and we were waiting for Chief Pat. We could see him coming across the river. In a few minutes we would say our final good-bye to him and head for distant Sisoguichic. None of us were in a talking mood.

The chief came directly to us. He, too, was silent and morose. I helped Estelle saddle her pack. Eppie assisted Jon with his. The chief picked up my heavy pack. I thought he was going to help me get into the web harness. Instead, he placed his arms through the straps, and hoisted the pack to his shoulders.

His action was indeed a surprise. He had never volunteered to carry one of our packs on any of the numerous trips we had made with him.

When everyone was ready, Chief Pat turned toward us and pointed toward the route of our departure. *"Mashi mabu!"* he commanded gruffly, and hurried down the trail.

I asked Eppie to tell the chief that I would carry the pack, and also that it was not necessary that he go with us. Chief Pat did not bother to answer. He only increased his already fast pace. I felt that the chief would stay with us until we reached a spring that was about three miles ahead, where he would give us his last good-bye.

At the springs, we quenched our thirst and refilled our canteens with fresh water. The chief refused to take my pack off his shoulders. He stood silently apart and watched us as we sat on the ground and rested. We prepared to leave the springs, and I looked at Chief Pat. I asked him for my pack, and he shook his head. As I had done at the start of our trip at Tehuerichic, I again carried Estelle's pack. Eppie relieved Jon of his burden.

Not so gruffly this time, the chief ordered *"Mashi mabu!"* I was touched by the little brown man's refusal to leave us and return to his home.

At the end of the fifteen-mile walk, where we were to meet the jeep from Sisoguichic, we

156

came to the inevitable and final parting. The chief could go no farther with us. The Indian and I were both awkwardly uncomfortable. Neither of us wanted to say good-bye.

I told my unhappy friend that, within two or three days, perhaps Father Laguna would fly me over the Tehuerichic area. We would fly low over his lean-to, and I would wave a greeting to him. This seemed to cheer the chief.

We started a handshake, and ended with our arms about each others shoulders in an unexpected embrace. The chief stepped back a pace, turned abruptly on his heel, and ran swiftly down the trail, with never a backward glance. I had a dull pain in my chest. The chief had not hugged me that hard.

We waited all afternoon for the jeep. At sundown we were still waiting, but not with any sense of alarm. We were, after all, in *mañana* land — the jeep would show up tomorrow. We pitched our tent, ate supper, and went to bed. It rained all night.

The rain stopped the next morning before noon. Shortly after noon, the belated jeep and its harried driver came hurtling out of a nearby canyon. We loaded aboard, and the rusty and dusty vehicle clawed, bounced, and roared its way back to Sisoguichic.

157

The morning after our return, Father Laguna consented to fly me over the route my family and I had taken to Tehuerichic. Not only would I see my friend Chief Pat again, but I would also have the good fortune to photograph the breathtaking view of the barranca country from the air.

We took off from the tiny airstrip at seven o'clock in the morning, when the air was comparatively smooth and cool. Father Laguna, one of the best of pilots, explained that the hours between early morning and late afternoon were extremely dangerous to fly in, particularly in takeoffs and landings. In recent years several pilots, unaware or disdainful of these hazards, attempted to land at the short strip at Sisoguichic. The results were fatal.

The little Piper Cub bounced and skipped along at a five-thousand-foot altitude. Sitting in the rear, I had the side window panel open, in order that I could take relatively unobstructed pictures of the fascinating panorama flowing below. The rush of wind past the ship was cold. Busy with my camera, I paid no heed to my chattering teeth.

The hodgepodge of crisscrossing, twisting canyons stretched onward as far as the eye could see. In the early morning sun, the highlighted crags and sharply etched ridge lines of the canyons

158

contrasted with the dark and shadowed depths of the lonely, brooding barrancas.

Studying the rugged, unfriendly land below, I found it difficult to accept the fact that my family and I had actually traveled so much of it on foot.

Father Laguna brought the plane to a low altitude as we approached Tehuerichic. The ship was about one hundred feet above the ground as it flew over the Río Conchos and skimmed with a roar over Chief Pat's flimsy lean-to. I could see the chief and members of his family running out of the shelter.

When we banked for a low return pass, Chief Pat was standing in an open area, a short distance from his home.

During the fleet moment the plane flew over, I was leaning far out my window. Chief Pat and I saw each other plainly.

As the plane swooped sharply upward, seeking altitude for the return flight to Sisoguichic, I looked back and saw the tiny, pathetic figure of my heathen friend. He was frantically jumping, and vainly reaching his arms toward a suddenly empty sky.

Thus ended our second year's venture into the lonely, sad land of the Tarahumara. Our return to the commonplace comforts and miracles of our modern world was not with the joyous

159

elation of a homecoming. Rather, it was one of mixed emotions, not the least of which was a strange feeling of guilt.

We would not forget Chief "Pat" Borrijic, and his brave, uncomplaining people — nor the terrible miseries that beset them.

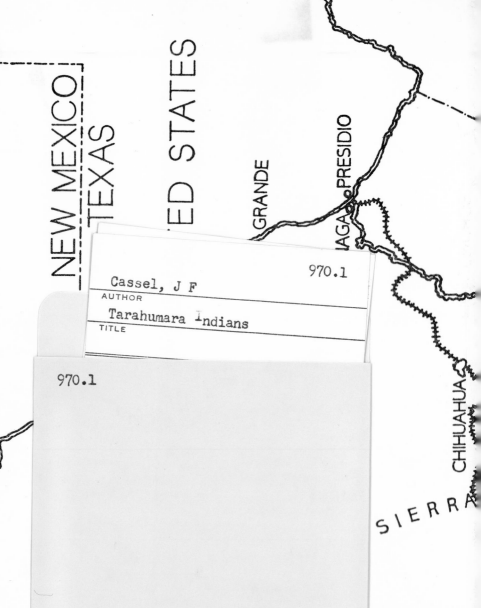

970.1

Cassel, J F

Tarahumara Indians

970.1

NEW MEXICO

TEXAS

ED STATES

GRANDE

PRESIDIO

CHIHUAHUA

SIERRA